The Gee Bee won air races,
but it killed pilots.

Fortunately, Jimmy Doolittle flew
the plane successfully.

A detail of the painting by
William S. Phillips of the air race
with the Gee Bee rounding the
pylon celebrates the extraordinary
acceleration in the development of aviation
achieved by the pilots who raced.

The detail from the above painting
that appears on the cover of
this edition is used by courtesy
of The Greenwich Workshop.

D0764786

On the afternoon of September 5, just before the aircraft were to line up for the Thompson, Doolittle's R-1 gave a fine demonstration of its skittish temperament. As it was being started up it backfired, the fuel in the carburetor caught it, and in a few moments the entire front end of the aircraft was ablaze. It was rapidly put out, with Doolittle assisting. No apparent damage had resulted, except to the crew's nerves, so Doolittle got back into it, started up again, and rolled out to the line where eight of the world's fastest landplanes were waiting.

Once in position, the pilots were given the stand-by, and the roar became deafening as the grass quivered against the ground behind them. Hall was the first to break, followed at ten-second intervals by Doolittle, Moore, Wedell, Haizlip, Ghelbach, Turner, and Ong. Bowen was left on the line in a storm of dust with engine trouble.

THE BANTAM AIR & SPACE SERIES

To Fly Like the Eagles . . .

It took some 1800 years for mankind to win mastery of a challenging and life-threatening environment—the sea. In just under 70 years we have won mastery of an even more hostile environment—the air. In doing so, we have realized a dream as old as man—to be able to fly.

The Bantam Air & Space series consists of books that focus on the skills of piloting—from the days when the Wright brothers made history at Kitty Hawk to the era of barnstorming daredevils of the sky, through the explosion of technology, design, and flyers that occurred in World War II, and finally to the cool daring of men who first broke the sound barrier, walked the Moon and have lived and worked in space stations—always at high risk, always proving the continued need for their presence and skill.

The Air & Space series will be published once a month as mass market books with special illustrations, and with varying lengths and prices. Aviation enthusiasts would be wise to buy each book as it comes out if they are to collect the complete Library.

THE GREAT AIR RACES

Don Vorderman

BANTAM BOOKS
NEW YORK · TORONTO · LONDON · SYDNEY · AUCKLAND

*This edition contains the complete text
of the original hardcover edition.
NOT ONE WORD HAS BEEN OMITTED.*

THE GREAT AIR RACES

A Bantam Falcon Book / published by arrangement with Doubleday

*PRINTING HISTORY
Doubleday edition published 1969
Bantam edition / August 1991*

Contents

Foreword

Don Vorderman, in *The Great Air Races*, gives an accurate and interesting account of three decades of air racing. Air racing, despite its hazard, contributed greatly to the development of both commercial and military aviation during this period. As Mr. Vorderman indicates, this contribution was almost a direct function of the money, brains and effort expended.

In 1925 a dollar was considerably larger than it is today and also much harder to come by. Neither our Army nor our Navy felt they could afford the expenditure of funds necessary for a new racer. Finally they agreed to go in together and split the cost. For a total expenditure of $500,000 they purchased four newly designed airplanes—the R3C's—and four newly designed engines—the Curtiss V-1400. One airframe was tested to near destruction which left three complete flyable airplanes and a spare engine. These airplanes were designed to fly either as landplanes with wheels or as seaplanes with pontoons.

Al Williams was acceptance test pilot for the Navy and I for the Army on this joint contract. We were both delighted with the performance and flying characteristics of these beautiful little aircraft.

This was the last year of "big" governmental support of air racing. The half million—big then—seems miniscule when the cost of developing a new aircraft and engine today is considered.

Air racing has largely outlived its usefulness as a stimulant to interest in aviation and in the development of improved aircraft and engines. I do, however, regret that our government did not continue to compete and improve our aircraft for a few more years, and sincerely hope that we will continue to do the considerable aeronautical research and development necessary to retain our regained lead.

J. H. Doolittle
9 February 1967

Author's Introduction

It is hardly news that the years from 1909 through 1939 were the most exciting in aviation history. This was partly because the art was so young and was growing so fast; but more particularly because the men involved in it, more or less by accident and with a good deal of luck, hit upon the most direct and effective method of cultivating it. The method was air racing.

During this thirty-one-year period (with the exception of the war years) virtually every new development in aeronautics was first tried out on racing or record-breaking aircraft. The results were often immediate triumph or tragedy, and it was by such means that aviation raised itself from the status of an intriguing novelty to the enormously elaborate science it is today.

This book covers the histories of all of the five great air racing classics—the Thompson, Bendix, Schneider, Pulitzer, and Gordon Bennett races, in addition to certain less historic contests which relate to them. The reader will not find them dull.

Why do these accounts end in 1939? I think this is probably justifiable, and it is certainly realistic. The reasons are simple enough. In 1946, after the tremendous strides made in the aeronautical sciences during World War II, attempts were made in the United States to recapture the glory of the prewar years, but to just about everyone's surprise it was gone. Flying the deadly offspring of World War II—Corsairs, Lightnings, Mustangs, etc.—brave and skillful men still gambled against the same odds, some winning, some dying, but the old sense of contributing to the advancement of aviation had disappeared.

But make no mistake, these postwar races were *fast*. So fast that it seemed nearly impossible to lay out a course so spectators could see the aircraft for more than a few brief seconds per lap. As a result, the public interest which was so essential—now that there was no longer active sponsorship by government and industry—began to decline, and in 1949, after a final accident in which several lives were lost, unlimited air racing was stopped.

But man's drive to prove himself cannot be bottled up quite so easily. Once again unlimited air racing has been taken up in the United States, smoothly run and with careful attention now given to the public's safety. One can only wish the pilots and organizers well, for despite the fact that there is little that air racing can now bring to aviation, it still continues to be what it has always been—the most exciting, deadliest sport of them all.

D.L.M.V.
New York City

The Gordon Bennett Races

By 1909 the Gordon Bennett trophies had been the most sought-after prizes in automobile and balloon racing, and with good reason. The competition was fierce and truly international, the events were staged with a great deal of flourish, and the publicity given them in newspapers and magazines was enormous. It seemed appropriate, even inevitable, that a similar prize be set up for air racing. James Gordon Bennett, Jr., son of the pioneering newspaper publisher and a pretty smart businessman himself, was more than equal to the occasion.

In a sense, air racing really began with the second airplane, but it wasn't until Bennett offered up his trophy that air racing began to make history. From that day aviation was given direction, and its future was secure. Even by 1909 there were still a lot of people around who had serious doubts about the intelligence of these birdmen and the practicality of their machines. No breed of skeptics ever disappeared so fast. The Gordon Bennett races were the first of the great air racing classics, but more importantly they were the prod that hurried aviation along that first bumpy flight out of confusion and into the realm of science.

Grand Semaine d'Aviation de la Champagne — 1909

The world's first international air races were held in late August of 1909 on the historic plain of Betheny, northeast of Rheims, where the troops of Joan of Arc had camped in 1429. News of this great event had spread all over Europe and by the middle of August the population of this beautiful city had swollen to more than twice its normal figure. Overjoyed proprietors of quaint inns and restaurants were gratefully skinning the visitors for all they were worth, and hotel rates were ten to twenty times the normal amount. On the whole, however, the visitors could take it. Princes, ambassadors, actresses, producers, Roosevelts, Goulds, Vanderbilts, and ordinary millionaires were everywhere, and somewhere among them (with few exceptions) were the pilots.

It was only to be expected that Europe's finest aviators would be there, headed by the great Louis Blériot himself. (Blériot's famous flight from France to England, with its profound significance for the British, had been made only a few weeks before, on July 25.) Among the others were Hubert Latham, Eugène Lefebvre, Count Charles de Lambert, English-born Henry Farman, and one lone American named Glenn Curtiss.

Altogether, some twenty-eight pilots had entered one or more of all the races scheduled, and the largest number of aircraft ever brought together (thirty-eight) were being made ready in nearby buildings or tentlike hangars—then called "aerodromes."

There were six events for aeroplanes scheduled to cover the eight-day meet:

The Grand Prix de Champagne, for the longest flight without alighting, with prize money totaling twenty thousand dollars donated by the local champagne growers.

The Prix de l'Altitude, to the competitor reaching the greatest height during the week, two thousand dollars.

The Prix de Passagers, to the entrant carrying the greatest number of passengers around one lap of the circuit, two thousand dollars.

The Prix du Tour de Piste, a sustaining prize for the fastest lap around the course each day, fifteen hundred dollars.

The Gordon Bennett Trophy, donated by James Gordon Bennett, Jr., now publisher of the New York *Herald*, for the fastest speed around two laps of the course, five thousand dollars and the trophy.

The Prix de la Vitesse, for the fastest speed over three laps of the course, four thousand dollars.

These last two events, along with the Grand Prix de Champagne, were the big ones, and there was no doubt in anybody's mind that new distance and speed records would be set. If anyone had suggested at the time that not one of them would be won by a Frenchman, he most probably would have been challenged to a duel, or at least locked up somewhere. But, as someone once observed, the unexpected always happens.

On the morning of the first day, Sunday, August 22, the great air meet was declared open and more than one hundred thousand visitors showed up to watch—in the rain! The weather was miserable, a layer of sticky, white mud covered the airfield and all roads leading to it, and local farmers were soon doing a land-office business hauling Rolls-Royces and Daimlers out of the muck. But the spectators bore the indignities willingly. They were well aware that they were about to witness the making of history.

The first day was to be devoted to qualification trials for the Gordon Bennett, the daily lap-speed prize, and a three-lap, 30 kilometer event.

Shortly after 10:00 A.M., Maurice Guffroy made the first attempt to get away. His little red R.E.P. monoplane furiously sputtered and struggled across the gummy field. Back and forth it went, but despite the roars of encouragement from the huge crowd, it wouldn't come unstuck. Guffroy retired in disgust when his fifteen-minute limit was up.

Then Blériot appeared on the field with one of his monoplanes and the crowd fell silent once more (most of those present had never even seen an aircraft before, hardly any a man actually in flight). Blériot, goggled and helmeted, gave a brief wave to the stands, opened the throttle of his 80 h.p. E.N.V. engine, bounced across the field for a few moments, and then gently slipped into the air. The cheering stopped almost at once, though, as Blériot's carburetor quickly failed under its diet of mud and water (it was still raining quite heavily). He returned after flying one side of the course and alighted safely — downwind.

Hubert Latham was the next away, also getting his Antoinette monoplane safely airborne, and also promptly putting down again with the same carburetor problems.

Captain Ferdinand Ferber's Voisin biplane was the next onto the field. As he was roaring through his take-off run his aircraft suddenly veered off course and made straight for the elegant gathering who were peacefully watching from under the umbrellas of the open-air restaurant in front of the grandstand. He hit the dining area smack in the center, amazingly without serious injury befalling anyone — except perhaps to their appetites.

The only really successful flight of the morning followed as self-taught pilot Eugène Lefebvre, who had been flying for only two months, actually managed to get his Wright biplane around the 10 kilometer course twice, the second lap made with a badly missing engine in a dangerously rising wind.

Obviously the weather was going to prevent the events being run off as scheduled, so at three o'clock that afternoon the contest committee met and selected Blériot and Lefebvre to represent France in the contest for the Gordon Bennett Trophy on Saturday.

At around six o'clock the wind and rain suddenly ceased, and almost at once there were more aircraft in the air at the same time and in one place than ever before. Hubert Latham was the first away, followed immediately by De Lambert's Wright biplane, Roger Sommer's Farman biplane, George

Cockburn's Farman biplane, and the Blériot monoplane of French sculptor Léon Delagrange. These were quickly followed by Henri Fournier's Voisin biplane, Lefebvre's Wright, Étienne Bunau-Varilla's Voisin biplane, Paul Tissandier's Wright, and the Voisin monoplane of Louis Paulhan. Captain Ferber had patched up his Voisin after hauling it out of the restaurant and was the last to join in the spectacle.

The spectators were simply agog, with as many as eleven aircraft laboriously buzzing around the course at once, though most of the flights lasted only a few minutes. (Blériot, who was as famous for his accidents as for his successes, ended up in a haystack this time, as did Fournier.) Latham put the crowd on the edge of their seats by flying past at the giddy height of 150 feet.

Lefebvre once more demonstrated his complete mastery of his Wright biplane, tossing the frail little craft about in front of the stands before gently coming to rest in front of the judges' enclosure. The judges fined him four dollars for "recklessness and daring." Only three entrants had managed to complete the required three laps. But that first day, at least from the spectators' viewpoint, had been an unqualified success.

As the day drew to a close, the official times stood as follows:

		3 Laps	Fastest Lap
Eugène Lefebvre	Wright biplane	26:42.6	8:58.8
Paul Tissandier	Wright biplane	28:59.4	9:25.2
Count de Lambert	Wright biplane	29:02	9:33.4
Hubert Latham	Antoinette monoplane	—	9:47
Louis Paulhan	Voisin monoplane	—	10:50
Roger Sommer	Farman biplane	—	11:24
George Cockburn	Farman biplane	—	11:44
Étienne Bunau-Varilla	Voisin biplane	—	11:56

The day had clearly been a walkover for the Wright machines, and the brothers who had given powered flight to the world were royally toasted (although they were not present) at a magnificent ball held in Rheims that evening. There was another American, Glenn Curtiss, who wasn't joining in the festivities. He was very busy back at the airfield putting the final touches to a remarkable little aircraft.

On the second day, Monday, August 23, the weather was as bad as ever, and though a moderate crowd of sixty thousand or so showed up they didn't see any flying until late in the afternoon. This was the first day of the flights for the endurance prize (the Grand Prix de Champagne), which would close on Friday evening. Wilbur Wright's endurance record of 2 hours, 20 minutes, 23.2 seconds (77.48 miles) set at Le Mans on the previous New Year's Eve was never in danger throughout the day, but the lap record for the meet was beaten twice.

By seven o'clock, broken, crumpled aircraft were scattered all over the course, and the attempts for the Grand Prix were as good as finished for the day. Blériot decided to have a shot at Lefebvre's lap record of 8:58.8 set the day before. He had the fastest of his five machines prepared, climbed aboard, and roared off down the course. Blériot scooted around the 10 kilometers in 8:42.4, setting a new world speed record at the staggering velocity of 42.87 m.p.h.

Glenn Curtiss had been preparing for a challenge like this, and his little Herring-Curtiss biplane (Herring was a business partner of Curtiss' back in the United States) was rolled out of its hangar and started up. Curtiss had also designed and built its 50 h.p. V-8 engine, and if anyone knew how to make it behave, he did. As Curtiss whipped around the first pylon the spectators were highly impressed by the smoothness with which the man and machine worked together, but they were awestricken when Curtiss' time was posted: 8 minutes, 35.6 seconds—seven seconds faster than the mighty Blériot! The world speed record now stood at 43.38 m.p.h.!

The day closed with many people reconsidering their predictions about the speed events to be held at the week's end.

On the following morning Blériot had his revenge with a new record lap at 8:04.4—46.18 m.p.h. Curtiss was grounded with carburetor problems all afternoon, but he promised to have a crack at it the next day.

French President and Madame Fallières arrived in the afternoon, accompanied by a rather nasty wind which unfortunately kept everyone grounded. Everyone but Louis Paulhan, that is. The hearts of the crowd were in their mouths as Paulhan's little Voisin valiantly staggered around the course for more than half an hour at a dizzy five hundred feet, at last setting down safely. Afterward, when asked why he had taken such a risk, he shrugged, amazed, "The President of the Republic was there! It was necessary!"

A very serious Glenn Curtiss soberly regards the camera just before setting out on his first trial flights at Rheims. (UPI)

On Wednesday there was still no improvement in the weather, and once more there were no flights until well into the afternoon when Paulhan, Latham, and Fournier tried for the endurance prize. Very soon both Latham and Fournier had disappeared, eventually arriving back on foot. Their machines were now resting in the "aeroplane graveyard," a hollow at the far end of the course where tricky wind currents had been collecting aircraft daily. Latham quickly rejoined the contest in a borrowed Antoinette but was down for good after two laps.

Though several others tried to get away, Louis Paulhan had the rest of the event to himself, coming down only when his fuel had run out, having set a new endurance record of 2 hours, 53 minutes, 24 seconds—81.35 miles.

As the weather had improved a bit, just about everybody managed a short flight after Paulhan was down. Curtiss tried to beat Blériot's new lap record, but only succeeded in beating his own, at 8:11.6. He would have to do a lot better than that.

On Thursday afternoon Latham at last managed to shake his bad luck and set up a new distance record of 95.92 miles, in 2 hours, 13 minutes, doing over fifteen laps of the course. He broke a wing upon alighting but was unhurt. Three spectators were injured, however, when Rougier's Voisin fell into the crowd.

Later on Blériot took his largest aircraft up, with a passenger, lost directional control on his approach, and ran into a fence. No one was hurt this time but the aircraft was all but written off. A few minutes afterward Curtiss tried again for a fast lap, only to put up his slowest time so far, at 9:31. Curtiss spent the night rebuilding the engine. Carefully.

As the last day dawned for the Grand Prix de Champagne, just about everybody who had anything left to fly had a go at it. The weather had cleared at last though it was still quite chilly. The favorites, Latham and Paulhan, were off first at about 11:00 A.M., followed by de Lambert, Tissandier, and the rest. Henry Farman took off in his lumbering Voisin at

Hubert Latham on his way to second place in the Grand Prix de Champagne, which netted him $5000. (Smithsonian Institution)

about four that afternoon and began quietly piling up laps. By this time Latham and Paulhan were down again, both having broken Latham's earlier record. Paulhan quickly refitted his Voisin with a bigger fuel tank and was off again. But he was no sooner back on the course when he had to fly his machine into the ground to avoid running into Delagrange's Blériot. Air traffic problems are not as modern as one might think.

All this time Farman was quietly circulating, and when he passed the two-hour mark the spectators, and the other pilots, began to take notice. Round and round he droned, first passing Wright's old mark, then those of Latham and Paulhan, on and on into the darkening sky. Flares were set up near the pylons, and motorists around the circuit obligingly turned on their headlights. Round and round. They were beginning to wonder if he had somehow become stuck up there, like some aerial Flying Dutchman, when he slowly began his descent at the end of his eighteenth lap and bumped awkwardly to a halt. His total distance was 111.85 miles in 3 hours, 4 minutes, 56.4 seconds, breaking all records for distance and endurance.

Farman was in no mood to appreciate his triumph. He was so stiffened by the cold he was literally unable to move, so he was carried back to his hangar where the champagne corks had already begun to pop. They soon warmed him up.

GRAND PRIX DE CHAMPAGNE

			Miles	
1st	Henry Farman	Voisin biplane	111.85	$10,000
2nd	Hubert Latham	Antoinette monoplane	95.92	$5,000
3rd	Louis Paulhan	Voisin monoplane	81.35	$2,000
4th	Count de Lambert	Wright biplane	72.03	$1,000
5th	Hubert Latham	(second flight)	68.93	$1,000
6th	Paul Tissandier	Wright biplane	68.90	$1,000
7th	Roger Sommer	Farman biplane	37.26	—
8th	Léon Delagrange	Blériot monoplane	31.05	—
9th	Louis Blériot	Blériot monoplane	24.87	—
10th	Glenn Curtiss	Herring-Curtiss	18.63	—
11th	Eugène Lefebvre	Wright biplane	13.04	—

On Saturday, the day of the Gordon Bennett race, the weather at last cleared up. Curtiss had tried out his aircraft just before dark on the previous day and had set his fastest lap yet, at 8:09.2. Still not enough to worry Blériot. The American worked his engine over again during the night, and this time it had to be right.

The following morning Curtiss wasted no time in finding out. Eleven minutes after the official starting time at 10 A.M., he was off on a trial lap. Whatever it was that he had done to his aircraft, it worked. He covered his test run in a time that sent Blériot scurrying for his goggles: 7:55.4.

As soon as Curtiss was down he had his tank topped up (he was carrying a smaller, lighter tank now), quickly slipped into a brown leather jacket, and tore off on the first lap of the race for the Gordon Bennett Trophy. His first tour was at 7:57.2, and on the second lap, with the throttle wide open now and the V-8 engine sounding magnificent, he dived over the finish with a time of 7:53.2—a total of 15:50.4, averaging 47.65 m.p.h. Curtiss landed, knowing that his engine could never take another lap like that last one. Whatever his time, it would have to stand now.

Blériot was after it right away, but he gave up his first attempt after a lap of 7:58.2. At twelve-thirty he tried again but could only get 8:14.4, and again just after three, giving up once more on his first lap. There was really no one else in the race now, and the honor of France was weighing heavily on Blériot's shoulders. At five-ten he made one last attempt (closing time was five-thirty). His first lap equaled Curtiss' best time at 7:53.2, but his engine had had enough and began to lose power. His time for the two laps was 15:56.2. Glenn Curtiss had won the first race for the Gordon Bennett Trophy.

Blériot bounded over to the startled Curtiss and gave him a resounding smack on each cheek, the huge grin under his handlebar mustache masking his bitter disappointment. Even Curtiss said afterward that he felt sorry for him.

But shortly afterward, Blériot went out and astounded everyone by setting up a new lap record in the Prix du Tour de Piste of 7:47.8, averaging 47.48 m.p.h., fully five seconds faster than Curtiss' best Gordon Bennett lap! And there was still the Prix de la Vitesse the following day . . .

The weather on the last day of the meet was beautiful; the kind of day the champagne country is famous for. But fate, for some, was as unkind as ever.

Glenn Curtiss' little biplane is led away from the grandstand after winning the first race for the Gordon Bennett Trophy for the United States. (Smithsonian Institution)

Curtiss really hit his stride now, and after a few trial runs he set up a time in the three-lap Prix de la Vitesse that was not to be equaled. His only real rival, Blériot, did one fast lap at 7:47, and then simply disappeared! A column of smoke began to rise in the distance. When they got to him he was found to be burned about his face and arms. Mercifully, his injuries were not serious.

When closing time arrived, the official times were:

PRIX DE LA VITESSE

Glenn Curtiss	U.S.A.	Herring-Curtiss	25:49.4	$4,000
Hubert Latham	France	Antoinette monoplane	26:33.2	—
Paul Tissandier	France	Wright biplane	28:59.2	—
Eugène Lefebvre	France	Wright biplane	29:01.5	—
Count de Lambert	France	Wright biplane	29:02	—
Hubert Latham	France	(second flight)	29:11.4	—
Louis Paulhan	France	Voisin biplane	32:40.8	—
Étienne Bunau-Varilla	France	Voisin biplane	42:25.8	—
Roger Sommer	France	Farman biplane	79:32.8	—

Latham easily won the Prix de l'Altitude with a pass at 503 feet, and Farman won the Prix de Passagers for carrying two people once around the course.

Curtiss went to Brescia the following week to demonstrate his now famous aircraft, and then returned to the United States to face a bitter legal battle with the Wright brothers. They claimed that his aileron device was an infringement of their wing-warping patents. It wasn't, but that's another story.

The Gordon Bennett Trophy — 1910

If the great benefits of international competition in aviation were to be first realized in France, the Americans were certainly anxious to show their enthusiasm for the idea. Oddly though, what should have been remembered as a milestone in the history of American aviation was reduced to the level of "the social event of the decade," due mainly to the ineptitude of the organizers and the travesty of sportsmanship displayed by a few of the pilots.

Though entries closed in March, the Aero Club of America had been advised of the teams intending to compete by the end of January. Britain and France were to field three entries each, and Italy had served notice that they intended to send one entry, but later withdrew.

The race was held at Belmont Park, Long Island, on the next-to-last day of a span of racing lasting from October 22 to October 30. Prize money totaling over eighty thousand dollars was to be offered, and though this looks like a lot of money it was spread pretty thinly over the nine-day meet. In view of the fact that the organizers were expecting, or at least hoping for, a daily attendance figure of around 175,000 to 200,000— at one dollar a head—it seems that they could have done a little better than this. (A Paris-Madrid race to be run in May of the following year carried a first prize of a cool fifty thousand dollars.)

As before, there were to be the daily, and in some cases hourly, prizes for altitude, distance, and speed, along with cross-country and passenger-carrying events.

There was another prize to be offered this year, but by the time the meet was over everybody would have been much happier if they had never heard of it. This was the "Statue of Liberty" prize of ten thousand dollars donated by New York financier Thomas F. Ryan. The prize was supposed to go to the competitor who would fly from the course out to the Statue of Liberty, around a balloon anchored at the site, and back to Belmont Park again, in the shortest time. It didn't turn out to be quite that simple, but more of that later.

Once more, just about all of the best pilots in the world were brought together at the Belmont Park races. The young flying machine had covered a lot of ground in the brief year since Rheims. Speeds were now nearly double those of the Champagne meet and altitude, distance, and duration flights that had set records the year before were now commonplace.

Arch Hoxsey was one of America's finest aviators in 1910, though he did not choose to fly in the Gordon Bennett race that year. (UPI)

One of the rare moments when Hubert Latham's V-16 powered Antoinette was running smoothly. During the course of the Gordon Bennett race, Latham spent more time on the ground than he did in the air. (UPI)

Among the more than forty pilots present were, from Great Britain: Claude Grahame-White, James Radley, W. E. McArdle and Alec Ogilvie; from France: Hubert Latham, Count Jacques de Lesseps, Alfred Leblanc, Émile Aubrun, René Simon, Roland Garros, and Edmond Audemars.

Understandably, the largest entry was from the United States. Among them were Charles K. Hamilton, John B. Moisant, J. Armstrong Drexel, Walter Brookins, Ralph Johnstone, and Clifford B. Harmon.

As there was quite a lot of aircraft-swapping going on during this meet, no attempt has been made here to specify all the entries of each competitor. The mounts of the various pilots will be mentioned only as they apply to specific events.

By the time the day of the Gordon Bennett had arrived several new American records had been set, but there had been no new world records so far. There had been several accidents, none of them serious, but the biggest excitement had been over Ralph Johnstone's attempt at the world altitude record on October 27. Although his effort was unsuccessful (at 8471 feet), the spectators were enormously impressed as his aircraft all but vanished in the cloudless sky above them.

Later in the same afternoon the competitors for the Gordon Bennett race were selected by the various teams.

The starting time for the event was set for 8:30 A.M. on Saturday, October 29, and the competitors would have seven hours to fly the course.

Grahame-White was the first to get away that morning, before a crowd of over thirty thousand. He flew his formidable

France	Alfred Leblanc	100 h.p. Blériot
	Hubert Latham	100 h.p. (V-16) Antoinette
Great Britain	Claude Grahame-White	100 h.p. Blériot
	James Radley	50 h.p. Blériot
	Alec Ogilvie	36 h.p. "C"-type Wright
U.S.A.	John B. Moisant	50 h.p. Blériot
	J. Armstrong Drexel	50 h.p. Blériot
	Walter Brookins	60 h.p. Wright "Baby"

100 h.p. Blériot over the 100 kilometers distance in 1 hour, 1 minute, 4.73 seconds, and without knowing it set an average speed of 66.2 m.p.h. that was not to be equaled.

Leblanc's Blériot was next to go out, and though his engine was no more powerful than Grahame-White's his aircraft was

Latham's Antoinette, here fitted with a V-8 engine, during the course of one of the earlier events at Belmont Park. (UPI)

James Radley's 50 h.p. Blériot is started up for one of the speed events earlier in the week. (UPI)

obviously a good deal faster. By the time Leblanc swept into his twentieth and last lap, over five minutes ahead of Grahame-White's time, the Englishman had abandoned any hope of winning. Then, only a few seconds from the finish line, Leblanc's engine suddenly sputtered and then fell silent. At the same moment a gust of wind threw him off course and slammed him into a telegraph pole, tearing his aircraft to shreds and snapping the pole in half. Leblanc wasn't seriously injured, but France's fastest entry was finished. (During this flight Leblanc had recorded a record speed of 68.20 m.p.h.)

Ogilvie's "C"-type Wright was out next, but was soon downed with a blown spark plug which kept it out of the running for nearly an hour.

Brookins was even more unlucky. His little 60 h.p. Wright "Baby" whipped past the stands at over 80 m.p.h. on its way to certain victory—when something came loose. He hit the ground at top speed directly in front of the grandstand and the aircraft literally disintegrated in all directions. After a few moments Brookins emerged from the wreckage, obviously in pain, staggered a few paces, and collapsed before the stunned spectators. He was quickly carted off in a horse-drawn ambulance to a field hospital that had been erected at the course. Except for extensive bruises he was found to be completely uninjured!

Hubert Latham's formidable V-16 Antoinette never got a chance to show what it could do, spending more time on the ground than in the air and eventually finishing the course at the rate of a fast walk.

Just before the seven-hour limit was up Drexel and Moisant made their bid to keep the Trophy in America. Seven laps later Drexel was out. Moisant did manage to complete the course, but was nearly an hour behind Grahame-White's time.

Great Britain, almost by default, and with a French aircraft, had won the Gordon Bennett Trophy.

Claude Grahame-White	100 h.p. Blériot	1:01:4.73	66.2 m.p.h.
John B. Moisant	50 h.p. Blériot	1:57:44.35	
Alec Ogilvie	36 h.p. Wright	2:06:36.69	
Hubert Latham	100 h.p. Antoinette	5:43:58.41	

On the following day, the awful Ryan "Statue of Liberty" farce took place. Grahame-White was the first to make the trip (about thirty-three miles) in 35 minutes, 21.3 seconds. Then Moisant and de Lesseps had a go, Moisant beating Grahame-White's time by forty-odd seconds. As the Englishman was preparing to make another attempt to hopefully lower his time, he was told that Moisant had lodged an appeal with the organizers to prevent Grahame-White from trying it again! What is even more remarkable is that the committee upheld Moisant's protest, even though the rules clearly stated that the entrants could fly the course at any time up to the close of the meet, the fastest one winning. The visiting Europeans, and most of the Americans, were absolutely stunned.

The meet ended in a state of complete chaos, with the presentation banquet boycotted by most of the pilots. An oppo-

Walter Brookins' Wright "Baby" makes a low pass for the benefit of news photographers on the day before the Gordon Bennett. (UPI)

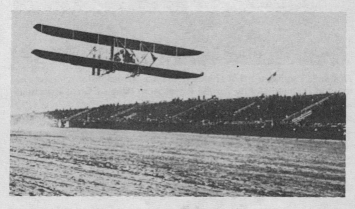

Brookins' Wright "Baby" only moments before it slammed into the ground directly in front of the grandstand. He was unhurt. (Smithsonian Institution)

sition party was given by Drexel, who saved what little there was left to be saved by declaring open warfare on the Aero Club of America.

Though the aeroplane had begun to grow up, some of the people connected with it clearly had not.

Dashing, handsome, rich Claude Grahame-White, after winning the Gordon Bennett Trophy for the Royal Aero Club of Great Britain at an average speed of 66.2 m.p.h. (UPI)

Moisant's Blériot sets out for the "Statue of Liberty" prize. (UPI)

The Gordon Bennett Trophy—1911

This year the Royal Aero Club felt that the Gordon Bennett race was now important enough in its own right to eliminate the necessity of cluttering up a whole week or more with endless, inconclusive and risky flying. There was usually some sort of flying meet going on on just about any weekend during the summer; more than enough to satisfy both the professional pilots and the enthusiasts.

The site chosen for this year's race was at Eastchurch on the Isle of Sheppey, just off the coast of Kent in the Thames estuary. The weather is generally better there than in other parts of Britain, and of course its convenience to London would ensure a sizable attendance. The date had been fixed for Saturday, July 1—as likely a day as any for good weather. A course of 150 kilometers (c. ninety-four miles), over twenty-five laps, was to be flown.

The pilots selected by the various teams were:

Great Britain	Gustav Hamel	100 h.p. Blériot
	Alec Ogilvie	50 h.p. Wright "Baby"
	Graham Gilmour	50 h.p. Bristol
France	Edouard Nieuport	70 h.p. Nieuport
	Robert Chevalier	70 h.p. Nieuport
	Alfred Leblanc	100 h.p. Blériot
U.S.A.	Charles T. Weymann	100 h.p. Nieuport

By the eve of the race representatives of all teams had made several trial flights around the course, and it seemed as though the Nieuports had it sewn up, with Weymann's Nieuport actually outrunning Nieuport's Nieuport!

Hamel had discovered that he would be nowhere in the race the following day if he couldn't find more speed—quickly. He asked Louis Blériot about it, and after musing over it for a while Blériot suggested he try chopping a few feet off the wings. This was to become the classic quick-cure for sluggish aircraft, a cure that was often to be much worse than the disease.

On Saturday morning Hamel tried his Blériot out with its new seventeen-foot wing. It was pretty hot to handle now, but he found that he could lap with Weymann and Nieuport, and that was all that mattered . . . or so it seemed.

Gustav Hamel standing by his 100 h.p. Blériot. Hamel was the first pilot to carry air mail in Britain. (Flight International)

Race day began looking dull and threatening, with a gusty wind thrown in to ruffle the pilots' nerves. Despite the gloomy outlook the spectators began arriving in hundreds, then by the thousands, and by early afternoon over twelve thousand had shown up to watch this third race for the Gordon Bennett Trophy. After the inevitable, but brief, shower the sun came out into a beautiful English summer sky.

The competitors were into it right away. Hamel was first off in his clipped-wing Blériot, but he didn't get very far. He just didn't have enough wing under him now and his aircraft fell out of the air at the first turn, slammed into the turf, and rolled itself into a ragged ball, stopping about 150 feet from the pylon. Hamel became the first of the very few pilots who would ever walk away from a ground-level high-speed stall.

Chevalier was next away, but his Nieuport soon developed carburetion troubles which finally forced him down again on his twelfth lap.

Weymann got onto the course just before Chevalier expired, and simply ran off with the race. Ogilvie, Leblanc, and Nieuport tried their best but the young American was too fast for them. Chevalier tried once more in another aircraft and was forced down in precisely the same spot as before, possibly wondering if he had been hexed.

1st	Charles T. Weymann	Nieuport	1:11:36.2	78.77 m.p.h.
2nd	Alfred Leblanc	Blériot	1:13:40.2	75.83 m.p.h.
3rd	Edouard Nieuport	Nieuport	1:14:37.4	75.07 m.p.h.
4th	Alec Ogilvie	Wright	1:49:10.4	51.31 m.p.h.

As the next Gordon Bennett race was to be held in the United States, the aero clubs of France and Britain were viewing the prospect with mixed feelings, remembering the disaster of the year before. They needn't have worried. Back in the States the critics had won the day and the Aero Club of America had been reorganized. Besides, the following year the Europeans would be bringing over a little bad news of their own.

Weymann prepares for one of his practice flights on the eve of the race. He appears quite confident here, and he had good reason to be. (Flight International)

Weymann and his Nieuport, moments before setting out into the Gordon Bennett race, which he won with ease. (Flight International)

The Gordon Bennett Trophy—1912

This year saw the Gordon Bennett Trophy go back to Europe again, but at least this time nobody was particularly surprised. In fact everyone concerned had quite a long time to reconcile themselves to the idea.

Jules Vedrines began writing on the wall with his new Gnome-powered Deperdussin in January when he set up a new record at 90.02 m.p.h. He steadily bumped it up five more times during the next six months, eventually arriving in the United States holding the world record at 106.12, also along the way having become the first man to officially exceed 100 m.p.h. in the air.

The Aero Club of America had announced back in March that no less than five countries would be sending entries to contest the Trophy this year—Belgium, France, Holland, Switzerland, and Great Britain. But as news of Vedrines' records appeared, one after the other the challengers found all kinds of reasons why they wouldn't be able to make it this year, until the only ones left in the race were the defending Americans who were now pretty far out on a limb, and the French who were about to saw it off.

Certainly the defenders didn't intend to take their punishment lying down. A syndicate had been formed in Chicago to supervise the construction of the American entry, and the Aero Club of America had announced it would pay ten thousand to fifteen thousand dollars for the design selected. This cash award turned out to be largely imaginary, but the constructors went ahead with the project anyway.

This American entry was built at the shops of the Burgess Company, in Marblehead, Massachusetts. Though they had been involved in the production of aircraft for several years, this organization was very famous at the time for another, quite unrelated, activity; the building of racing yachts.

Although they didn't seem to like the idea to begin with, the Burgess Company eventually gave in and the little monoplane was built, in about six weeks, to the designs of Glenn Curtiss.

The resulting aircraft looked suspiciously like one of the current Morane-Saulniers—but then the Morane looked an awful lot like last year's Nieuport. The Burgess machine had been designed around the most powerful aero engine then in existence: a double-row, 14-cylinder, 160 h.p. Gnome—only one of which had been built to order for this aircraft. It was really quite an impressive little machine, even though its designer seemed to have seriously understated the case for directional (yaw) stability. As it happened the aircraft wasn't ready in time anyway, possibly saving someone's neck (Glenn Martin had been selected to fly it in the contest).

When the French party arrived they were delighted with the layout of the course, and well they might have been. A brand new airport had been created for this event just outside Chicago, and the area had been so carefully seeded, watered, and rolled that it was more like a putting green with pylons than an airfield.

The French contingent consisted of Vedrines and Maurice Prévost, who would fly Deperdussins of 140 and 100 h.p., and André Frey, who was to fly a 100 h.p. Gnome-powered Hanriot. Several prominent French aviation personalities had also come along for the ride. Among them was Émile Aubrun, remembered from the Rheims and Belmont Park meets, and a certain M. Jacques Schneider, whose name was later to become the most famous of all in air racing.

The morning of September 9 dawned clear and cool, but surprisingly the temperature began to shoot up and by mid-morning it was blisteringly hot. It would probably have been impossible to fly the race but for a gusty, cooling breeze off Lake Michigan. Only about fifteen hundred spectators turned up to watch the race, this due mainly to the fact that the airport was practically inaccessible to anything but a private auto-

Vedrines' Deperdussin rounds one of the pylons at Chicago.

mobile or a horse. The daily papers hadn't helped matters either with their dismal prophecies that it would be more like a rout than a race. It was.

Ten minutes after the official starting time of 9:30 A.M., Vedrines lifted his beautiful little Deperdussin into the air and the fourth Gordon Bennett race was not only under way—it was over. Vedrines flew the entire course alone, completing it in 1 hour, 10 minutes, and 51 seconds, averaging 105.5 m.p.h. and finally coming to rest, after an extra lap, on the far side of the course. (Vedrines had heard about American souvenir hunters.)

Schneider was the first to congratulate him, draping Vedrines in a *Tricoleur* and walking him back to the crowd at the hangar. After sending off the necessary telegrams to France, they settled down to an *alfresco* lunch and waited to see what, if anything, the Americans would do.

Late that afternoon Paul Peck tried to get his 50 h.p. Nieuport into the race, a totally inadequate but nonetheless laudable attempt to show the United States flag. It was grounded with a flat tire.

Along about four-fifteen the French team decided that they may as well make it unanimous, so Prévost and Frey took their aircraft onto the course. Prévost's Deperdussin completed the distance in 1 hour, 15 minutes, 25 seconds. Frey, though it mattered little now, was downed with engine trouble at twenty-three laps.

After Prévost was down again, Vedrines went out once more, just to prove it hadn't been an accident, and established a new, official, world speed record at 108.18 m.p.h.

Though no one realized it at the time, the French had now become so much better than anyone else at this flying business that they were to dominate it for the next ten years.

Coupe d'Aviation Maritime Jacques Schneider

At the Gordon Bennett banquet on December 5, 1912, Jacques Schneider, heir to the Schneider steel and munitions factories at le Creusot, announced that he was introducing a new international trophy to promote the development of seaplanes. The series would be open to any club affiliated with the Fédération Aeronautique Internationale, and any country winning the Schneider Trophy three times within five consecutive contests would keep it, ending the series.

It wouldn't be too unreasonable to say that Schneider's announcement has had a telling effect on the lives of all of us. It might even be said that as a result of Schneider's offer, the Germans began to lose World War II two years even before Sarajevo.

Why?

Because of the Spitfire, and because of the Rolls-Royce *Merlin* that powered it—two deadly devices that contributed as much as any Allied war machines, and probably more, to Hitler's repeated decisions to postpone his invasion of Britain. Both were direct outgrowths of the Schneider races, and what they accomplished, together and separately, against the mercilessly concentrated might of the Luftwaffe from the time of the Battle of Britain and onward could, under any other circumstances, seem almost unfair to the Germans.

Certainly, there was a breed of superlatively brave and skillful men who were the real source of Britain's air strength— the "thousand British boys" that, in Churchill's judgment, probably saved civilization. But all their bravery and skills would have been impotent without the right instruments to demonstrate them, and we can all be thankful that they existed at the right time and in the right place.

But what does a ''wealthy sportsman's'' banquet in 1912 have to do with *die Götterdämmerung* in the 1940s? Perhaps nothing . . . perhaps everything. Perhaps the outcome would have been the same in the long run . . .

Perhaps . . .

The magnificent Coupe d'Aviation Maritime Jacques Schneider. English aviators called it the ''Flyin' Flirt.'' (Smithsonian Institution)

The Schneider Trophy— 1913

The first Schneider Trophy contest was held, sensibly enough, at Monaco, on the morning of April 16, 1913. It had been arranged by the Aero Club de France and was at first only one of a series of flying contests for ''waterplanes'' which spread over two weeks. The race was to be run over twenty-eight laps of a 10 kilometer (6.21 mile) course, and was held in perfect Monegasque weather.

Only two countries competed: France and the United States. After the preliminary trials there were four entrants left, three from France and one American.

Maurice Prévost	Deperdussin	160 h.p. Gnome	France
Roland Garros	Morane-Saulnier	80 h.p. LeRhone	France
Dr. Gabriel Espanet	Nieuport	100 h.p. Gnome	France
Charles T. Weymann	Nieuport	100 h.p. Gnome	U.S.A.

As in the Gordon Bennett races the competitors were sent away singly, and the first to go, at about 8:05 A.M., was Prévost in his Deperdussin. Espanet was next up at eight-fifty, and Weymann last at nine-fourteen. Garros had attempted to follow Prévost but he was unable to get off after puncturing a float and had to retire.

Dr. Espanet had displayed a very seaworthy craft with stepped floats and he consistently put up the fastest times until a broken oil line forced him down after 70 kilometers. This left Prévost and Weymann to fight it out, and it was with great relief that the French saw Weymann alight three laps from the finish with a leaking oil line: he had been lapping several seconds faster per lap. Prévost continued on to complete the course alone in 2 hours, 50 minutes, 47 seconds.

After Prévost had been down for about an hour, somebody remembered the rule that stated that the competitors must cross the finish line while still airborne. Prévost had crossed it on the water!

Prévost grabbed a pair of goggles, dashed off for his aircraft, dived into it, started up, and tore off the water, whipped around in a tight circle and crossed the line, this time officially. It is for this reason that his speed for the race has been recorded at 45.75 m.p.h., actually well below his Deperdussin's stalling speed!

France's rather hollow 1913 Schneider victory was none-theless the cause for a sudden and sustained blossoming of elaborate plans for French seaplane racing, but it would all be to no avail. France was never to win the Schneider Trophy again.

Some entrants in the seaplane races at Monaco. 1. Gaubert's Farman. 2. Weymann's Nieuport. 3. Garros' Morane-Saulnier. 4. Bregi's Breguet. (Smithsonian Institution)

Maurice Prévost's Gnome-powered Deperdussin seaplane, winner of the first race for the Schneider Trophy. (Smithsonian Institution)

The Gordon Bennett Trophy—1913

The 1913 Gordon Bennett race was little more than a repeat performance of the 1912 race, staged for the benefit of the European audience. Once again pilots of England, Belgium, America, and this time Italy and Germany, had gone through the motions of announcing their intention to compete, but on the appointed day of the sacrifice only one of them had shown up: Henri Crombez, of Belgium.

The contest was held on Monday, September 29, in beautiful weather, once more outside the city of Rheims. Maurice Prévost had taken over the world speed record on June 17 at 111.74 m.p.h. He had raised it again during the Gordon Bennett trials on September 27 to 119.25, both records being made with his Deperdussin, now powered by a double-row 160 h.p. Gnome.

In addition to Prévost, Émile Vedrines (brother of Jules) was to fly a 160 h.p. Gnome-powered Ponnier-Pagny, and Eugène Gilbert's 160 h.p. LeRhone-powered Deperdussin rounded out the French team.

Crombez had been selected by ballot as the first set out around the course. Shortly after 9:00 A.M. on this fine autumn morning he lifted his Deperdussin off the field and onto the first of the twenty 10 kilometer laps. There were no fireworks or "incidents" while the Belgian was aloft, and he completed the course in 1 hour, 9 minutes, 52 seconds—actually slightly faster than Vedrines had been in Chicago in 1912, but everybody knew it wouldn't be enough this year.

Prévost went out about an hour after Crombez had landed, and promptly nailed down the Gordon Bennett for another year.

Maurice Prévost with his 160 h.p. Gnome-powered Deperdussin, a combination which dominated air racing in 1913. (Smithsonian Institution)

His first lap set a new world speed record at 126.67 m.p.h. He eased off a bit after that and sailed around without missing a beat for the rest of the distance, completing it in 59 minutes, 45.6 seconds.

Gilbert was next, and he seemed to be creeping after the blistering pace set by Prévost, though he too was considerably faster than last year's winner.

Émile Vedrines was last away, and was actually only slightly over a minute slower than Prévost.

1st	Maurice Prévost	Deperdussin	0:59:45.6	France
2nd	Émile Vedrines	Ponnier-Pagny	1:00:51.4	France
3rd	Eugène Gilbert	Deperdussin	1:02:55.4	France
4th	Henri Crombez	Deperdussin	1:09:52	Belgium

It might be mentioned that the share of the prize money of F. 100,000 put up by Armand Deperdussin had recently and very suddenly disappeared (attached by the French government) when Deperdussin was discovered to be dealing in funny stock certificates.

C'est la guerre!

The Schneider Trophy—
1914

April 20, 1914, will forever be recorded as the prophetic day when Britain graduated permanently to the rank of a major international air power. On that day, Howard Pixton, flying a seaplane version of the brand-new Sopwith "Tabloid," so thoroughly trounced his opposition, so completely shattered existing notions of what a seaplane should be able to do, that several of his waiting competitors, after watching him scorching around the course, didn't even bother to challenge him.

Britain had certainly produced noteworthy aircraft before the "Tabloid," but this win marked the beginning of a trend that was later to demonstrate her complete dominance over the high-speed aircraft of the rest of the world.

If the credit for this first portentous victory were to be given to one man, he would be T. O. M. Sopwith. His great gifts in aeronautical design, coupled with his knack for putting the right people in the right places, were to be heavily relied upon during the coming war. The Sopwith "Pup" and "Camel" would leave their indelible stamp on aviation, and on history.

There were eight entrants lined up bright and early on that clear Monday morning, and although Pixton's little Sopwith had looked quite promising during its trials, the other entrants felt it was still a very open race. They were about to have their ideas changed.

At the start were:

Dr. G. Espanet	Nieuport	France
A. Levasseur	Nieuport	France
Roland Garros	Morane-Saulnier	France

Pixton's Sopwith underway during the race. It was the first British aircraft to win an international event.

Howard Pixton	Sopwith	Great Britian
John (Lord) Carbery	Deperdussin	Great Britain
Ernest Burri	Franco-British	Switzerland
Charles T. Weymann	Nieuport	U.S.A.
William Thaw	Deperdussin	U.S.A.

Victor Stöffer of Germany had intended to enter an Aviatik, but crashed before the contest and was unable to compete.

Although the rules stated that the competitors had "between 8:00 A.M. and sunset" to fly the course, the echo of the eight o'clock starting gun had hardly died out when it was replaced by the buzz of two Gnome rotaries as Levasseur and Espanet bounced off the water and banked into their first lap of the course. Pixton's Sopwith was next at eight-five, followed by Burri's graceful little Franco-British flying boat. Carbery was the last to take off, and the first to retire—on his first lap—wisely decided to avoid the dangers of low-level racing in Janoir's completely unfamiliar, borrowed Deperdussin.

It was soon all too obvious that Pixton's Sopwith was burning up the course, averaging around 90 m.p.h. per lap. This speed put everybody else completely out of the picture, and Pixton maintained it in fine style right through to the end. In fact, he completed two extra laps in order to have his speed officially recorded for 300 kilometers. It came to 86.8 m.p.h., a new world record for seaplanes.

It was argued by some at the time that the Sopwith did not represent an entirely British victory as it was fitted with a nine-cylinder Gnome *Monosoupape* rotary engine manufactured in France. This point seems somehow offset by the fact that during the latter half of the race it was, perhaps resentfully, running on only eight cylinders.

Sadi Lecointe's Spad arrived at Bournemouth but was kept out of the race by leaky floats. (Flight International)

After watching Pixton's tremendous performance, Garros, Weymann, and Thaw decided that it would be a waste of time to compete. Espanet had retired after sixteen laps with engine trouble and Levasseur was similarly afflicted one lap later. Burri had sportingly continued and, after putting down briefly on his twenty-third lap to take on more fuel, he completed the course to secure second place at an average of 51 m.p.h.

So the possession of the Schneider Trophy passed to Great Britain, and would remain there, uncontested, for the duration of World War I, which was now only nine weeks away.

The Schneider Trophy— 1919

The contests for the Schneider Trophy were immediately taken up again after the war, the first one being held, according to the rules, in the country of the previous winner. This third Schneider was held at Bournemouth, then a fashionable resort on the south coast of England. The course was over ten laps of twenty nautical miles each, and extended from the start at Bournemouth Pier, out to Swanage Bay, then to Hengistbury Head and back to Bournemouth Pier.

This was to be the first of three consecutive Schneider races that would rank among the dullest air races in history, but behind the scenes there was *plenty* of excitement.

A decision of No Contest was finally given for this event. The conflicting opinions that arose out of it would probably furnish enough material to fill a book by themselves, but the perspective of time seems to show us that this is the way it happened . . .

By anyone's standards the weather that September morn was at least tolerable. The sea was glassy smooth, but this was actually a decided disadvantage for some; the flat-bottomed floats on some of the aircraft were better suited to slightly choppy seas which actually lessened the shock of landing. There were patches of fog lurking about in the area which were so thick that visibility was down to about forty feet inside them, but it appeared to be staying away from the race area. Heavy, unpredictable gusts of wind completed the picture. It wasn't much of a day for an air race.

After the trials had been held on September 8 three entries from England, two from France, and one from Italy were to compete for the Trophy.

The French had had appalling luck. Two Nieuports had crashed in France while under test, a third one went down in the Channel, and a fourth Nieuport arrived in England only to ram a buoy while alighting. It was taken into Saunders' yard and several teams worked over it in shifts to get it ready. There were two more Nieuports to be flown by Henri Malard and Jean Casale, as well as the Spad of Sadi Lecointe.

Entries from Spain and Belgium had been promised, but were withdrawn, and Captain Hammersley's Avro "Puma" was eliminated in the trials.

Throughout the midday hours of September 5 both the contestants and the crowd watched the distant fog shift, thin out, seem to lift for a time, and then roll back in again. Then, at around two-thirty (official starting time), the worst happened— a thick, soupy mist descended around everything.

The remaining French entries made the most of the delay by taking their light-weight, leaky floats apart for repairs, under the impression that the start had been put forward to six o'clock. It must have come as a mighty shock to them when, at around five, the British officials, without any warning, decided to start the contest!

First off was Vincent Nicholl in his Fairey III. Next, and incidentally out of correct starting order (and without even receiving a starting signal!) was Commander Hobbs in the Supermarine "Sea Lion." Harry Hawker followed in his very fast Sopwith, he also without receiving any apparent starting signal.

Then Lieutenant Guido Janello, the last competitor (due to the non-start of the furious French team who were left high and dry with repairs) taxied his Savoia S-13 up to the start and calmly waited for the flag to drop, after which he roared off into the fog, leaving the damp spectators to ponder over what was turning out to be an incredibly mismanaged race.

After a short time Nicholl's Fairey appeared out of the mist, flying *across* the course, and hurriedly sat down in the sea, seemingly intent on remaining there. Immediately afterward Hawker's fierce Sopwith materialized, charging along in the opposite direction! After circling over the start for a few min-

Commander Hobbs' Supermarine "Sea Lion." Hobbs was forced down by fog during the race, and the "Sea Lion's" hull was punctured by a submerged object before he could get off again. (Flight International)

utes and fiddling with the throttle, he also decided to call it a day.

There had been no sign of Hobb's Supermarine since his takeoff, and some concern was developing about his welfare. It was later learned that he had punctured a float when he was forced down by fog at Swanage.

During all this confusion Janello was neatly observing the rules and going around like clockwork, each lap being around ten minutes, plus or minus a few seconds. He was now the only competitor left in the race.

After the "contest" had dragged on for a while, what must have been the equivalent of today's leather jacket set made an appearance. Several private aircraft materialized over the crowd and proceeded to show off, fortunately without incident. Then the reserve Avro piloted by Captain Hammersley joined in and did a few *hors concours* laps of the circuit for the benefit of the spectators.

Janello, racing only against the falling darkness, doggedly completed the required number of laps, and then brought his Savoia S-13 gently to rest near Bournemouth Pier. Just about everyone present was of the opinion that he thoroughly deserved the Trophy for his remarkable courage and skill, to say nothing of his eyesight. But later that evening as congratulations were being showered on him, word arrived from one of the mark boats on Swanage Bay that they hadn't seen his Savoia even once during his entire flight!

Pandemonium reigned! It was certainly clear that Janello had been circling *something* from the regularity of his lap times. It appears that there had been another boat on the course, naturally where it didn't belong, and Janello had been meticulously circling the wrong one!

Many strong words and letters were exchanged, with the Italians finally, and understandably, lodging a formal complaint with the F.A.I. about the management of the race.

Although the race was eventually declared No Contest, there was no doubt in anybody's mind as to who was the moral victor. After "discussions" between the Royal Aero Club and the F.A.I., it was decided to entrust the organization of the next Schneider Trophy race to Italy and to award them the "custody" of the Trophy, after which everyone seemed to breathe a little easier.

The Schneider Trophy— 1920

The 1920 Schneider race was the second of three rather unfortunate events in the series.

This year the Italians were left to compete among themselves for the trophy, the British and French having failed to arrive, though both had planned to enter, while the Americans ignored the Schneider races altogether.

The 1920 flyover was held just outside the lagoon at Venice, over ten laps of a triangular course of twenty nautical miles to the lap.

On September 18 Lieutenant Luigi Bologna, the only entrant, successfully completed the seaworthiness trials in his Savoia S-19. On the following day he made an attempt to fly the course in extremely bad weather, only to be forced down after five laps as his aircraft was becoming uncontrollable in the rapidly worsening wind conditions.

On September 22 he made another try, and after completing the course in 2 hours, 10 minutes, 35 seconds, he was declared the winner at an average of 107.2 m.p.h.

The Schneider Trophy would remain in Italy for another year.

The Gordon Bennett Trophy—1920

After an interval of seven years, what was destined to be the last of the great Gordon Bennett air races was held on September 28, 1920 near the little Seine-et-Oise town of Etampes, about thirty-five miles south of Paris.

Inevitably, the pressures of World War I had brought about a dramatic change in aviation. Those rickety, cranky machines of 1913 had now become tough, dependable aircraft which could produce astonishing performance by prewar standards, but they were also much more demanding of their pilots. Flying was now a very serious business.

The course for this year's Gordon Bennett was to be over 300 kilometers (about 186 miles), consisting of three trips from Villesauvage Airport at Etampes out to the town of Gidy, some fifty kilometers distant, and back. This clearly promised to be the most hotly contested air race ever held, and the entrants from Great Britain and the United States were just as determined to carry off the trophy as the French were to keep it; and if France could win it for the third successive time it would be theirs permanently, and the Gordon Bennett races would be ended.

The most impressive collection of racing aircraft ever assembled were being readied for this last Gordon Bennett:

Great Britain

L. R. Tait-Cox	British Nieuport "Goshawk"	320 h.p. A.B.C.
F. P. Raynham	Martinside "Semiquaver"	300 h.p. Hisso
Harry Hawker	Sopwith	450 h.p. Bristol

Roland Rohlfs with the "Texas Wildcat." The aircraft is shown here with its original "slow" wing. The crude suitcase-shaped radiators were fitted as a last resort when the pressures of time prevented the installation of wing radiators. (Smithsonian Institution)

France

Bernard de Romanet	Spad	300 h.p. Hisso
Sadi Lecointe	French Nieuport	300 h.p. Hisso
Paul Kirsch	French Nieuport	300 h.p. Hisso

U.S.A.

R. W. Schroeder	Verville-Packard	638 h.p. Packard
Roland Rohlfs	"Texas Wildcat" (Curtiss)	400 h.p. Curtiss C-12
Howard Reinhart	Dayton-Wright RB-1	260 h.p. Hall-Scott

Unfortunately, even the most careful planning cannot meet every contingency, and several of the fastest entries were eliminated before race day. Hawker's Sopwith, the same aircraft that might have won the Schneider the year before, became snared in a financial and legal tangle back in England and had to be withdrawn. Great Britain's Tait-Cox Nieuport didn't arrive at the course within the stipulated time due to a maddening hassle with British Customs at Lympne and was disqualified.

What might have been a very serious accident eliminated Rohlfs' "Texas Wildcat" shortly before the race. Americans had heard so much about the smoothness of French airfields that it was decided to eliminate shock damping units on the

"Wildcat" undercarriage in an attempt to save weight. It only remains to be said that when Rohlfs touched down at Ville-sauvage Airport after an early test flight he hit a ditch *very* hard and the "Wildcat" was destroyed. Rohlfs suffered little more than some impressive bruises and the "Cactus Kitten," a sister ship also built by Curtiss for this event and held in reserve, was promptly withdrawn.

Howard Reinhart's very advanced Dayton-Wright RB-1. But for a snapped rudder cable, and despite the fact that it was considerably underpowered, it might well have won the race. (UPI)

Kirsch's Nieuport recorded the fastest lap of the race on his first tour, but was forced down with oiled-up plugs on his second lap. (UPI)

The impressive, but very heavy, Verville-Packard VCP-1 was a great disappointment to the American team. It had been fitted with a new, and untried, high-compression engine on race day, and its mechanics didn't have time to properly adjust the ignition timing and carburation. (UPI)

F.P. Raynham's Martinside "Semiquaver" being run up before the start. (UPI)

On the morning of race day the weather was foul—thick fog with a smattering of rain. As the hours passed the assembled crowd (incidentally, probably the smallest ever to watch a Gordon Bennett race) and competitors alike were hoping that the weather would improve, but by midday it seemed obvious that it wouldn't, so the mechanics began running up the engines for last-minute tuning adjustments while the pilots wished each other luck and made off to their respective mounts. As the engines were being fired up, as though by prearrangement, the fog lifted immediately and the temperature began to fairly shoot up.

If the practice sessions during the preceding days indicated anything at all it seemed pretty certain that the Americans would run away with the race. Schroeder's thundering Verville-Packard was packing over twice the horsepower of most of the other entries, and Reinhart's Dayton-Wright, though comparatively low on power, was probably the cleanest, most technically advanced aircraft in the world. Even with the withdrawal of the Curtiss-Cox racers, the Americans seemed to have the race in the bag.

Kirsch was first away in his Nieuport at 1:25 P.M., and as he completed his first lap 21 minutes, 29 seconds later his teammate Romanet joined him on the circuit. Kirsch's first lap turned out to be the fastest of the day at 172.9 m.p.h., but this was little consolation to him as his plugs began to oil up at the end of his second lap, forcing him to call it a day.

As Kirsch was putting down Lecointe was getting on to his first lap, and as it turned out, he was on his way to winning the last of the Gordon Bennett races while the American threat simply evaporated under the suddenly beaming autumnal sun.

Schroeder's formidable Verville-Packard, which before the race had looked and sounded as though it would effortlessly swallow up the opposition, at first refused to start and then encountered carburetion problems as soon as it was airborne. For the race the aircraft was fitted with an untried, high-compression engine. Great sheets of flame began to pour from the exhaust, startling the crowd and doubtlessly Major Schroeder also. With the risk of fire there was no alternative but to retire.

Howard Reinhart's superb Dayton-Wright developed steering problems at the end of its first lap. An inspection revealed that the port rudder cable had snapped, obviously scuttling any hopes of continuing.

The English were no luckier. Their last remaining entry, Raynham's Martinside "Semiquaver," lasted only a lap before its oil pump failed.

So what had promised to be a fiercely contested race turned out to be a disappointment to all. All, that is, except the French, who simply walked away with it. Despite the fact that his opposition practically fell apart in the air Lecointe justly deserved his win. From the moment he took off until he put down again 1 hour, 6 minutes, 17 seconds later, his performance was flawless. His engine never missed a beat and his flying was superb. To put the cap on this French victory, the only other aircraft to complete the course was De Romanet's Spad. Two weeks later De Romanet boosted the world speed record to 181.87 m.p.h.

With this win France now gained permanent possession of the Gordon Bennett Trophy, and there was an aura of sadness throughout the festivities that evening with the realization that an historic era in aviation was at an end.

But on the other side of the Atlantic another was just beginning.

Lecointe's Nieuport is run up by mechanics before the race. (National Archives)

The Pulitzer Trophy

On the afternoon of August 12, 1919, the news was released that the brothers Ralph, Joseph Jr., and Herbert Pulitzer, publishers of the New York *World* and the St. Louis *Post-Dispatch*, had received the approval of the U.S. Government to sponsor a series of international air races in the United States. Within a few hours the news was all over the American aviation industry. Nothing on this scale had ever been seen outside Europe, and it seemed that at long last the American public would be given a chance to see for itself the tremendous strides that had been made since those first faint flutterings at Kitty Hawk. Make no mistake, American aviation desperately needed favorable public opinion.

After the pioneering work by the Wrights and Glenn Curtiss, fumbling American governmental mismanagement and Pecksniffian budgeting had ultimately resulted in European supremacy in the air. America still possessed the talent all right—some of the finest pilots in the world, and designers who were on a par with the best anywhere—but even in those days it took more than talent and wishes to build an airplane. It took money, and a lot of it. Experimental aircraft are very, very expensive. It was for this reason that the U.S. Government's official recognition of the forthcoming Pulitzer series was a highly welcome straw in the wind, and it was the first hint of the strong financial support that was to come.

Although this series would be open to entrants from any nation desiring to compete (with the observance of certain safety regulations), it was expected that it would be dominated by American, Service-type aircraft. While this was to be so to some extent, there were some startling surprises in store.

The Pulitzer Trophy—
1920

As much as twenty-four hours before the start of this first Pulitzer contest a huge crowd had begun to condense around Mitchel Field, near Garden City, Long Island. By some accounts over forty thousand spectators were to witness America's first big air race on that Thanksgiving Day, November 25, 1920.

It was certainly a perfect day for an air race, with the temperature around 50 degrees, a smooth, steady wind of around 12 to 15 m.p.h., and a very high overcast which would make for fine spectating. As an indication of the importance accorded to this event, among those present were Secretary of the Navy Daniels, General Pershing, Anthony H. G. Fokker and, inevitably, air-power advocate Billy Mitchell, then a brigadier general.

A widely varied assortment of aircraft had been prepared for this first Pulitzer, and although a staggering sixty-three entries had been accepted, only thirty-four actually flew the course. It would be to no purpose to describe each entry, as most of them were fairly commonplace and quite outclassed by a small number of much more interesting aircraft.

Captain Harold Hartney, the World War I ace and popular aviation figure, was to fly a Thomas-Morse Scout MB-3 which had unofficially beaten the American speed record earlier in the year. It was powered by a 300 h.p. Wright power plant.

Bert Acosta, a civilian with a rapidly growing list of successes and already the possessor of an enviable reputation as an enormously gifted pilot, was to fly a privately entered Italian Ansaldo "Balilla."

Lieutenant Corliss Moseley was to fly the very promising Verville-Packard which had hopefully had the bugs chased out of it since its poor showing at the Gordon Bennett race in France two months before.

Lieutenant St. Clair Streett, fresh from his epic New York-Alaska-New York flight, was to pilot a standard Army Air Service Orenco Model D, also powered by a 300 h.p. Wright.

The Chief Navy threat was Lieutenant B. G. Bradley's Loening Special, not a terribly exciting machine to look at, but its appearance belied a performance potential that put it very strongly in contention for an outright win.

The booming engines of the early starters began clearing their throats for this first big air race in America, and finally at eleven-twenty the first signal was given and Captain Hartney's Thomas-Morse roared into the air, gained altitude, and then shot across the starting line and onto its opening lap. In rapid succession the remaining thirty-three entries were flagged away, the last being the much-fancied Verville-Packard flown by Moseley.

In what seemed like no time at all Hartney flashed around the home pylon again ending his first lap. It soon became clear that this would be a race between his Thomas-Morse and Moseley's Verville-Packard. The aircraft were visible for a considerable distance as they approached and left Mitchel Field, but it was impossible without a stopwatch to say which was faster. The Verville-Packard seemed to be just a little quicker down the straights, but its high wing-loading made it something of a handful at the pylons, while the nimble Thomas-Morse would flick around the corners and scoot away without seeming to use up an unnecessary inch.

The question was settled when Moseley shot across the start-finish line at the end of his fourth lap exactly 44 minutes, 24.5 seconds after he first crossed it, beating Hartney's time by only two and a half minutes. Hartney's performance becomes quite remarkable when one considers that he was giving away over three hundred horsepower!

Acosta, flying what many felt was an outclassed Ansaldo, took third place, less than seven and a half minutes behind the winner. St. Clair Streett was only a few seconds behind Acosta, securing fourth.

The unfortunate Bradley, whose Loening had been up among

the leaders throughout the race, was forced to retire when only a mile from the finish, with a leak in his cooling system.

It later transpired that there had been an error in the course measurements, and the speeds usually recorded for this event are therefore somewhat optimistic. Elapsed times, of course, remain the same. The corrected speeds for the top placings are:

Moseley	Verville-Packard	156.5 m.p.h.
Hartney	Thomas-Morse	148.0 m.p.h.
Acosta	Ansaldo "Balilla"	134.5 m.p.h.
Streett	Orenco Model D	133.0 m.p.h.

On the following day Moseley took the Verville-Packard up again, this time with his eye on a new world speed record. Bernard de Romanet, flying a Hispano-powered Spad, had two weeks before hit 192.01 m.p.h., the highest official speed then recorded. The Verville-Packard couldn't make it though, the timed runs over the measured mile averaging 186 m.p.h.

Moseley's Verville-Packard which had appeared at the Gordon Bennett races in France two months before, where it laid an egg. Newly styled the "R-1," it was now a much more dependable aircraft. (UPI)

The first Pulitzer was by all accounts a tremendous success, from everyone's standpoint. The fact that there had been so many aircraft on the course at one time without a single incident made it very clear to even the stuffiest conservatives that aviation was no longer the risky business it once had been. The cautious, unpredictable American public almost overnight became a stanch supporter and champion of aviation. As an exultant Glenn Curtiss happily declaimed after the 1920 Pulitzer, "The public, at last, is interested in the airplane."

The Schneider Trophy—
1921

The fifth Schneider Trophy contest was something of a failure, as had been the two before it. Once again Great Britain had declined to enter, and although Frenchman Sadi Lecointe had actually arrived at Venice with a very fast 300 h.p. Delage-powered Nieuport, a structural weakness in its undercarriage eventually forced its withdrawal.

So once again the Italians were left to fight among themselves for the Trophy, and from an impressive entry of nineteen air-craft the three fastest were chosen by the race committee to make the official flights:

Arturo Zanetti, who was to fly a Macchi M-19 powered by a huge twelve-cylinder Fiat V-12 which pounded out a walloping 720 h.p.

Giovanni de Briganti, who had entered a Macchi M-7 powered by a 200 h.p. six-cylinder Isotta-Fraschini.

Piero Corgnolino, who would fly another Macchi M-7 fitted with a 250 h.p. Isotta six.

The contest, if not uneventful, was something of an anti-climax, with both Zanetti and Corgnolino retiring, leaving De Briganti to complete the course alone at 117.8 m.p.h.

The one incident that caused some excitement during the race was when Zanetti's machine dramatically caught fire in the air. He managed to put down safely, neither he nor his riding mechanic being scratched or scorched.

For the second successive contest Italy had won the Schneider Trophy unopposed, if not unchallenged. She needed to win it only once more during the next three contests and she would have it permanently, and the Schneider Trophy contests would be ended.

Arturo Zanetti flew this Fiat-Macchi M-19 in 1921, and was on his way to certain victory when his machine caught fire in the air. Neither he nor his riding mechanic were injured. (Smithsonian Institution)

The Pulitzer Trophy— 1921

The most significant feature of the second Pulitzer was the clear demonstration of how participation in open competition inevitably leads, through experimentation, to improvement. This classic rule must apply where one's chosen field is aeronautical engineering, burgling, or girls, and it was demonstrated very plainly at the '21 Pulitzer.

The U.S. Navy, no doubt piqued by its poor showing at Mitchel Field the previous year, had commissioned the Curtiss Aeroplane Company to design and construct two aircraft to represent the very latest design techniques in high-speed flight.

The order was issued late in May, and an amazing two months later, on August 1, the first Curtiss Navy Racer, designated CR-1, was rolled out of the Curtiss works at Garden City, Long Island for its first trials. The services of Bert Acosta, who had placed third in the previous year's Pulitzer, had been engaged by the Curtiss Company to test these new machines.

This sleek little biplane with its superb Curtiss CD-12 direct-drive engine belting out over 400 horsepower was the first of a brilliant series of Curtiss racers that were to quickly establish the United States as a world leader in high-speed aviation.

Only six aircraft participated in this second Pulitzer, being held in Omaha, Nebraska, quite a comedown from the previous year's entry—but there was no shortage of excitement.

Although completed in record-making time the new Curtiss Navy Racer was in danger of not competing. The Navy Department for some reason now refused to accept responsibility for either the expense of competing, or the potential loss of the aircraft altogether. Fortunately the necessary strings were pulled and the aircraft was "loaned" to the manufacturer for this event, and test pilot Acosta was on hand to fly it.

The "Cactus Kitten," sister ship to the "Texas Wildcat," a non-starter at the previous year's Gordon Bennett, was also entered and was to be flown by Clarence Coombs. Both of the Curtiss-Cox specials had been entered for this event, but the officials frowned strongly on the very high landing speed of the biplane "Wildcat" and refused to let it compete. (The rules stated that no entry would be accepted which landed at more than 75 m.p.h.) The bright red "Kitten," formerly a monoplane, was hurriedly fitted with a new triplane wing layout which brought its landing speed down into the seventies, but it was still an awful handful to fly. It was by far the favorite of the crowd.

The remaining four entries were as follows:

Lieutenant Colonel Harold Hartney, who took second spot the previous year, would fly a Thomas-Morse MB-7 powered by one of the new 400 h.p. Wright V-8's.

The R-1 and R-2 under construction. The R-1 is nearer the camera. The upper wing of the R-2, with built-in radiators, rests on stands in the background awaiting installation. Both aircraft were finished nine weeks to the day after the Navy ordered them. (U.S. Navy)

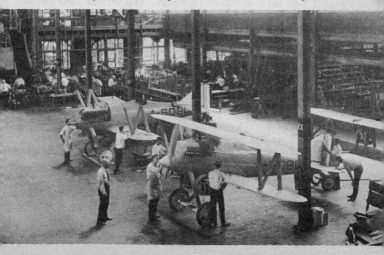

Bert Acosta tried out the "Kitten" after it had been converted into a triplane in 1921. One short flight convinced him that he would never willingly set foot in it again. He chose to fly the R-1 in the 1921 Pulitzer and only narrowly avoided being beaten by the "Kitten."

Lloyd Bertaud would fly an Ansaldo "Balilla," refitted with a 400 h.p. Curtiss C-12, sporting a huge four-bladed propeller.

James A. Macready was to fly a Thomas-Morse MB-6, also driven by a new 400 h.p. Wright V-8.

James Curran would fly an S.V.A.-9 (Savoia-Verduzzio-Ansaldo) powered by a 225 h.p. S.P.A. engine.

Originally to be held in Detroit, the site for this second Pulitzer had been shifted to Omaha. The course laid out for the event consisted of five laps of a 30.7-mile circuit, adding up to 153.5 miles. Triangular in shape, it extended from the airport at Omaha out to the town of Carson, Nebraska, then across the state line and Missouri River to Loveland (!), Iowa, and back to Omaha.

The weather was beautiful that November 3, without a cloud in the sky, and with the temperature at ground level at around 48° F.

At the toss-up to determine the starting order, it fell to Bert Acosta to lead the way. His silver-gray Curtiss fairly leaped into the air and a few seconds later flashed over the starting line at something like 200 m.p.h. Bertaud's four-bladed Ansaldo followed Acosta three minutes later. The third man to go was Clarence Coombs, and the crowd gave the little red projectile a wild cheer as it blasted by onto its first lap. Before Coombs was out of sight Acosta had returned, covering his first 30-mile lap in an amazing 9 minutes, 40 seconds.

Colonel Hartney was to follow Coombs but was having fuel feed problems at the start, so Curran was sent off in his S.V.A.-9 and was followed shortly by Macready's Thomas-Morse MB-6.

From the moment Coombs' "Cactus Kitten" joined Acosta's Curtiss Navy Racer on the course, it was clearly a race between the two of them. Coombs would gain on the straights, while Acosta would make up time again with his pylon-rattling turns. Acosta flew at treetop level for most of the race while Coombs kept the "Cactus Kitten" a good deal higher, sensibly feeling his way in his first flight in this temperamental, if not downright hysterical airplane.

The argument was settled, though, when Coombs chased Acosta over the finish line a scant 1 minute, 58 seconds behind the Curtiss Navy Racer. Acosta's speed of 176.7 m.p.h. was also a new world record for closed course racing.

Macready and Bertaud followed at 160.7 and 149.7 m.p.h.—remarkably close behind, considering the blistering pace, the actual time between first and fourth place being only 9 minutes, 22 seconds. Curran had been forced to land with engine problems at the end of his third lap.

Bert Acosta with the first Curtiss Navy Racer, outside the administration building at the Curtiss factory on Long Island. The Pulitzer Trophy is standing near the wheel. (Smithsonian Institution)

After all the other aircraft were down, Hartney was still trying to get his fuel system to feed properly and was informed by the Contest Committee that he would have twenty minutes to get going or would be disqualified. A frantic eighteen minutes later Hartney crossed the line and was off on his first lap, which he never completed. Twenty minutes later a call came in from a farmer near Loveland to say that an aircraft had crashed on his property and that the pilot was severely injured. Hartney was rushed to the farmhouse and examined by a physician who diagnosed a broken hip and serious internal injuries. It was later determined that his injuries were not as severe as had been thought, and Hartney was expected to be up and about again in a few months.

The Schneider Trophy— 1922

But for the industry and initiative shown by Hubert Scott-Paine of Supermarine Ltd. the Schneider contests might have ended this year with Italy gaining permanent possession of the trophy. Virtually unopposed in 1920 and 1921, the Italians, far from indulging in idle fly-arounds, had developed some of the fastest flying boats in the world, and with each year that passed they were becoming harder to beat. Government sponsorship of Schneider teams was still a beautiful dream, and it was a considerable commitment and risk—not to mention the expense—on the part of Scott-Paine which resulted in the Schneider Trophy returning to Great Britain.

This sixth contest was flown at Naples on August 12 over a course of 230 nautical miles, being the aggregate of thirteen triangular laps of 15.3 miles each. Only four aircraft flew the course.

The single British contestant, Henry Biard, had brought over a Supermarine Sea Lion—a Sea King series flying boat with clipped wings and a 450 h.p. Napier ''Lion'' replacing its standard 300 h.p. Hisso.

Arturo Zanetti was to fly a Macchi M-17 powered by a 250 h.p. Isotta-Fraschini.

Piero Corgnolino was to pilot a Macchi M-7, powered by a 250 h.p. S.P.A., and Arturo Passaleva would be flying a very promising-looking new Savoia S-51 powered by another 300 h.p. Hisso. All of the Italian entries were of the flying boat type.

Two French C.A.M.S. flying boats had also been entered

but an Italian railroad strike prevented their arriving in time to compete.

The morning of August 12 dawned clear and cool, a beautiful Neapolitan day.

As before, the competitors were free to start any time they wished, and Biard, playing a waiting game, let the other three go first. The Italians weren't the least bit worried about Biard now, as his practice laps had finally settled around 135–140 m.p.h., a good 10 m.p.h. too slow.

It must have come as something of a shock to Corgnolino, who was the first to be aware of it, when Biard's Supermarine shot past him so fast he might have been tied to a post. Biard then mixed it up for a few laps with the other two, finally taking the lead and cutting a few 160 m.p.h. laps before easing off to win in a canter. One of the Italians, Passaleva, might otherwise have caught—possibly even passed—Biard, but a splintered propeller forced him to keep his revs down.

The victorious team received a tremendous welcome on their return to England, with mayoral receptions, speeches, and the like, but the Trophy's stay in England, this time, was to be a short one. Plans were already under way that would result in her losing it again the following year.

The Pulitzer Trophy— 1922

The story of the 1922 Pulitzer might be compared with that of a kind but homely maiden aunt who attends a ball as a chaperone and ends up marrying the handsome young prince.

In less than a week of competition the fierce little Curtiss racers rewrote the world-record speed charts from top to bottom, running off with absolutely everything from the one-kilometer to the 200-kilometer honors. The habit of playing second best is a hard one to shake off psychologically, and it was very clear that the Americans were more than a little startled over what they had done. As William D. Tipton, a highly respected aviation journalist, wrote at the time, "Frankly, we didn't believe we had it in us!"

This much was true, although it was expected that some of the fastest times yet seen in closed course racing would be established. (It was announced on the day of the race that Lieutenant Russell Maughan had recorded a startling but unofficial 220 m.p.h. twelve days before, in one of the spanking-new Curtiss Army Racers. This was something like 15 m.p.h. over the current official world record now held by Sadi Lecointe.)

Several months before the projected date for this third Pulitzer, the Curtiss Aeroplane Company had submitted designs to the Navy Department which embodied the results of a year's worth of research and refinement of the previous year's Curtiss Navy Racers. The Navy turned them down. Forgivably, they didn't see the purpose in financing the construction of two very expensive aircraft to compete against the ones they already

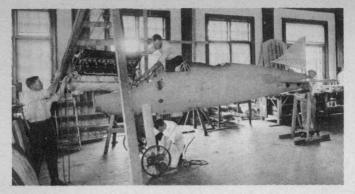

One of the Curtiss R-6's under construction. The monocoque plywood fuselage, developed from a process first devised in France, weighed only 127 pounds. (U.S. Army)

had. Valuable time was wasted while the Curtiss Company looked around for private interests to sponsor the construction of these new designs—without result.

For a while it seemed they would never be built, and then the obvious happened—the Army stepped in. Not only did the Army want these aircraft built, but they wanted them built *right now*, in time to be fully flight tested and on the line at the start of the forthcoming Pulitzer races in Detroit.

The Curtiss Company was given an impossible three months to construct these two highly complicated aircraft. (Though quite similar in outward appearance, they were much more complex internally than the previous year's models.) Working night and day, the Curtiss staff made it, though, amazingly with time to spare. Enough time in fact for Lieutenant Maughan to set his unofficial record.

By the morning of October 14 a huge crowd of over seventy-five thousand had gathered along the ten-mile leg from Selfridge Field to Gawkler Point, near Detroit, to watch what would turn out to be the world's fastest air race. The shape of the course was triangular, roughly equilateral, with each leg around ten miles long, and most of it over water. The contestants were to fly five laps, which added up to 155.34 miles. (The course was laid out to metric measurement to simplify computations should world records be broken.)

A new trophy was offered at the 1922 races. Named after General Billy Mitchell's younger brother who had died in France during World War I, the John L. Mitchell Trophy was open only to members of the 1st (and only) Pursuit Group of the U.S. Army Air Service. Surprisingly, it proved to be as fiercely contested as the Pulitzer itself, though the aircraft themselves were not quite as spectacular. Flown just before the Pulitzer race, this year's Mitchell Trophy was contested by six standard service Thomas-Morse MB-3's over four laps of the Pulitzer circuit. Lieutenant Donald Stace got home first on this hard-fought and well-flown event, with a winning speed of 148 m.p.h.

It had been decided that the Pulitzer would be run in three heats to limit the number of aircraft on the course at one time. The heats were made up as follows:

Heat 1

Captain F. P. Mulcahay	Thomas-Morse MB-7	U.S.M.C.
Lieutenant S. W. Callaway	Booth "Bee Line" Racer	U.S.N.
Lieutenant E. H. Barksdale	Verville-Sperry	U.S.A.A.S.
Lieutenant F. B. Johnson	Verville-Sperry	U.S.A.A.S.

Heat 2

Lieutenant R. L. Maughan	Curtiss Army Racer	U.S.A.A.S.
Lieutenant L. J. Maitland	Curtiss Army Racer	U.S.A.A.S.
Lieutenant H. J. Brow	Curtiss Navy Racer	U.S.N.
Lieutenant A. J. Williams	Curtiss Navy Racer	U.S.N.
Lieutenant L. H. Saunderson	Navy-Wright "Mystery"	U.S.M.C.

Heat 3

Captain Corliss Moseley	Verville-Packard	U.S.A.A.S.
Lieutenant E. C. Whitehead	Loening-Packard	U.S.A.A.S.
Lieutenant L. D. Schulze	Loening-Packard	U.S.A.A.S.
Lieutenant C. L. Bissell	Thomas-Morse MB-7	U.S.A.A.S.
Captain F. O'D. Hunter	Thomas-Morse MB-7	U.S.A.A.S.
Captain St. Clair Streett	Verville-Sperry	U.S.A.A.S.

Promptly at 1:00 P.M. the first heat was away. Although it was expected that these would not be the fastest entries in the race, this heat was of particular interest in that all but one of the aircraft featured the newfangled retractable landing gear,

Lieutenant L. H. Saunderson's Navy-Wright "Mystery" sesquiplane being run up by mechanics before the start. It was forced down with engine trouble. (UPI)

Mulcahay's Thomas-Morse being the only one in this heat with fixed wheels. The crowd was tremendously moved at the sight of all these airplanes flying about without any wheels at all. Even some of the pilots viewed this new contrivance with mixed feelings, and not without reason. Bert Acosta, after having made a recent trial flight in one of the Booth Racers, had "landed" it without bothering to crank the wheels down.

Everybody remembered this time, however, but the two Verville-Sperrys were the only ones to complete the required five laps. Both Mulcahay and Callaway suffered breakdowns in their oil systems and retired safely on their third laps.

Now came the moment that everyone had been waiting for. The crowd was tense with excitement as the time at last approached for the second heat to go. Then all at once, the air over Selfridge Field was filled with thunder as five of the most advanced aircraft engines in the world began to bellow their impatience to be off.

The signals were given and, in what seemed like only a few seconds, the roar had died away again as the five aircraft vanished down the course. Seventy-five thousand pairs of eyes now began to search the silent sky for a sign of the first aircraft to reappear, ending its initial lap.

A little after eight minutes later, some of the sharper eyes picked out a speck on the horizon. Most dismissed it, and continued to wait out the ten minutes that the faster ones were expected to take. But the speck remained, and grew, and then another appeared, and then another! Suddenly the sky was full of Curtiss Racers!

First Maughan's Curtiss Army Racer whipped around the pylon in a ninety-degree bank and blasted away onto its second lap. About thirty seconds later Maitland followed in the sister ship. Then, within twenty more seconds, both Curtiss Navy Racers had shot past with Saunderson's Navy-Wright howling in their slipstream. *This* was an air race! Maughan's time for his first lap was an astounding 9 minutes, 3.2 seconds, representing a lap average of 204.8 m.p.h.

During the next thirty-six minutes every world closed-course speed record up to 200 kilometers was blasted to smithereens, and many of the spectators were having a hard time convincing themselves it was really happening.

There was no doubt though by the time Maughan sat his Army Racer down again, that it *had* happened. Maughan had covered the five laps at an official 205.8 m.p.h. To bring the point home even more fully, the first *seven* aircraft in the final placings exceeded the current world record speeds for closed course racing.

Lieutenant Lester Maitland beside the Army's Curtiss R-6 with which he captured second place in the Pulitzer at 198.8 m.p.h. (Smithsonian Institution)

The Loening-Packard aircraft of Whitehead and Schulze shortly before the start. (UPI)

Captain St. Clair Streett's Verville-Sperry which was forced out of third heat with a seized engine. (UPI)

This second heat was a very hard act to follow, but the pilots in the third heat wasted no time in getting on with it. Moseley's Verville-Packard VCP-1—the winning combination in 1920—was the fastest in this heat, and though his speed was far below that of the newer Curtiss Racers, his speed in this heat (178.9 m.p.h.) secured sixth place over-all, a highly creditable performance for a three-year-old.

Even more remarkably, there were only four retirements from this race: Mulcahay and Callaway in the first heat as already mentioned, Saunderson, who had to ditch his Navy-Wright in shallow water on the fourth lap of the second heat with engine trouble, and Streett who was out with a seized

Lester Maitland's D-12-powered Curtiss R-6 which took second place at 198.8 m.p.h.

engine on his last lap in the third heat, none of these retirements being attended by serious damage or injury. It was, in short, an almost perfect air race.

The final placings were as follows:

1st Lieutenant R. L. Maughan   Curtiss Army Racer 205.8 m.p.h.
2nd Lieutenant L. J. Maitland   Curtiss Army Racer 198.8 m.p.h.
3rd Lieutenant H. J. Brow   Curtiss Navy Racer 193.8 m.p.h.
4th Lieutenant A. J. Williams   Curtiss Navy Racer 186.7 m.p.h.
5th Lieutenant E. H. Barksdale Verville-Sperry   181.2 m.p.h.
6th Captain Corliss Moseley   Verville-Packard   178.9 m.p.h.

Just to drive the point home, four days after the race General Billy Mitchell himself took the winning Curtiss Army Racer up and set a new, official world record for the kilometer of 222.97 m.p.h., with one run clocked at 243 m.p.h.

American aviation had finally arrived.

The Schneider Trophy— 1923

The 1923 Schneider contest was the final proof that America— or, more accurately, the Curtiss Company—was now building the fastest, most reliable high-speed aircraft in the world.

A sort of *per pecuniam ad astra* situation was taking hold in aviation, where the success realized were in direct proportion to the amount of money spent in development and research. This rule had only recently met with grudging acceptance by the U.S. Government, and this largely to the credit of General Mitchell. In a few short years, however, the British and Italians were to exploit this rule so effectively that their high-speed aircraft would completely outclass the best that the rest of the world would field against them. But their day was yet to come.

In the spring of 1923 the F.A.I. and the Royal Aero Club were informed that the United States intended to compete in the 1923 Schneider race. An early roster of those intending to take part comprised three entries from Great Britain, four from France, four from America, and two from Italy.

Quite a few were eliminated for various reasons before the contest. Flight Lieutenant W. H. Longton's Sopwith-Hawker, which might very well have given the Americans a run for their money, had thrown its spinner and crash landed near Brooklands on its last test flight as a land plane. On a trial flight American Lieutenant A. W. Gorton's very promising Navy-Wright NW-2 had thrown one of its three propeller blades which punctured its port float, causing it to sink on alighting. The Italians withdrew their two entries a week before the race, and one French machine, a Blanchard, did not appear.

The remaining entries to take part in the navigability trials at Cowes, Isle of Wight, on September 27 were as follows:

Great Britain

Henry C. Biard	Supermarine "Sea Lion III"	450 h.p. Napier "Lion"
R. W. Kenworthy	Blackburn "Pellett"	450 h.p. Napier "Lion"

U.S.A.

Paul Irvine	Curtiss CR-3	465 h.p. Curtiss D-12
David Rittenhouse	Curtiss CR-3	465 h.p. Curtiss D-12
F. W. Wead	Navy TR-3-A	265 h.p. Wright E-4

France

Jean Duhamel	Latham	Two 400 h.p. Lorraine-Dietrich
Claude Hurel	C.A.M.S. 38	360 h.p. Hispano-Suiza
Pellitier d'Oisy	C.A.M.S. 36-A	360 h.p. Hispano-Suiza

Entrants were now required to "taxi across the starting line and then ascend, alight and taxi over two marked distances of ½ mile each at a speed greater than 12 knots per hour, fly a short marked course, then descend, taxi across the finish line, tie up and lie moored for six hours unattended."

Kenworthy's "Pellett" was the first to undertake the trials. His aircraft had a rather bad history of misbehaving while seaborne, and it lived up to its reputation admirably. While on its initial run just before leaving the water it began to "porpoise" violently, stuck its nose into the sea, flipped over, and promptly sank with the unfortunate Kenworthy still at the controls. Several fast power boats raced to the site where bubbles were appearing and began to circle. Hopes that Kenworthy would appear were at last fulfilled as he bobbed to the surface, very wet inside and out, and lucky to be alive. He had been suddenly plunged underwater without an instant's warning, and trapped there for over a minute. He was fished out and carried off by one of the launches, sadder and wiser.

Biard's "Sea Lion III" was next, and it breezed through its trials without a hitch.

The two American CR-3's followed Biard. These were the

R. W. Kenworthy, an instant before his aircraft plunged under water. (Flight International)

The Curtiss Navy Racer R-2 was the first aircraft to be fitted with wing radiators (on upper wing) that worked. (Smithsonian Institution)

same two aircraft that had been built by Curtiss to the order of the U.S. Navy back in 1921, Acosta winning the Pulitzer of that year in one of them, and the pair of them placing third and fourth in the following year. Floats had been fitted, engines changed, and the ingenious Curtiss wing radiators installed on both; otherwise they were more or less as originally designed. Both were running the new Reed dural propellers. Each completed the trials successfully, though Irvine was required to repeat a few stages, because of a misunderstanding, before the judges were satisfied.

Wead's TR-3-A was to go next. He was no sooner under way when his Wright E-4 threw a propeller blade which chopped off the end of his port float. The entire undercarriage collapsed instantly and the aircraft rolled over and sank. Wead was unhurt.

The French team was next in order, and unfortunately Duhamel's 800 h.p. Latham also eliminated itself right at the start by shearing its starting gear. Hurel went out in his C.A.M.S. 38 and made up for at least some of this disappointment to the French supporters by recording a flawless performance in the trials. It was perhaps just as well, because the last French entry, Georges Pellitier d'Oisy, absently rode his C.A.M.S. 36-A into a moored steam yacht on the way to the start.

After all the remaining machines had successfully completed the six-hour mooring test they were put onto their dollies, drawn into S. E. Saunders' huge hangar, and bedded down for the night.

From the original twelve aircraft which had been officially entered, only four were left to take part in the speed trials on the following day.

September 28 dawned clear, cool, and still. The Solent was like a millpond. It was an altogether perfect day for the speed trials. If anything, it was a little too perfect to suit Biard in the lone British entry, as it was assumed that his Supermarine would have been much better able to cope with a rough sea than the obviously faster Curtiss CR-3's. But as the eleven-o'clock starting signal drew nearer, it became quite clear that the weather would remain perfect for the rest of the day.

Both Rittenhouse and Irvine were speeding toward the starting line as the last few seconds before eleven ticked away. They shot over the line and left the water a few moments after the hour, turned 180 degrees in opposite directions to keep out of each other's way, and tore off down the first leg of the course. For the first time their CD-12's were wide open and the ease with which they seemed to spring into the sky gave cause for considerable gloom in the other camps.

Biard was scheduled to go at eleven-fifteen. After impatiently dawdling about until his time came up, he began his run toward the starting line. At that moment the hundreds of spectators gave a great gasp of surprise as Rittenhouse's Curtiss suddenly shot past overhead, going a great deal faster than

Wead's TR-3-A after its undercarriage collapsed. (UPI)

The French entries during the mooring tests. Duhamel's twin 400 h.p. Latham is in the foreground, the C.A.M.S. flying boats of Hurel and Pellitier d'Oisy at the left. (Flight International)

anyone imagined it could. Irvine was only twenty seconds behind him. They were both out of sight again before Biard got onto the course. It was obvious to all that if they kept going at this rate they would run away with the race—which is precisely what they did.

Hurel took off at eleven-thirty to join the other three, but his entry was now more in the nature of a sporting gesture than anything else. He retired on his second lap with engine trouble after covering his first lap at 130.4 m.p.h.

After Hurel's retirement Biard and the two Americans were left to fight it out, though there seemed little doubt as to the outcome by then. The two Curtiss racers were recording laps of over 170 m.p.h., while Biard's dogged though vastly outclassed ''Sea Lion'' was getting around at about 152 m.p.h.

Eventually Rittenhouse slammed past the finish line at the end of his fifth lap after setting up a record speed for the Schneider series of 177.38 m.p.h. and a world record for seaplanes to boot. Irvine, whose engine had gone slightly out of tune, followed his teammate a few minutes later, recording 173.46 m.p.h.

When Biard crossed the line at the end of his last lap, his elapsed time was nine minutes, twenty seconds behind the winner's, which worked out to a quite creditable 151.16 m.p.h.

So the 1923 Schneider contest ended with the United States winning it for the first time. The cruiser U.S.S. *Pittsburgh* had been ordered to act as a sort of supply ship for a party that was later held at the Royal Marine Hotel at Cowes for all those involved in the race. One English journalist present was highly

Rittenhouse tears across the Solent on the way to America's first victory in the Schneider Trophy races. (Flight International)

impressed by the fact that a dry ship from a dry country could produce a party with such a remarkable wetness! A hilarious time apparently was had by all, although the English did admit that the dramatic presence of the Schneider Trophy in the foyer of the Royal Aero Club would be sorely missed by the members. They had become so used to hanging their hats on it on the way to the bar.

Irvine at speed rounding one of the mark-boats. (Flight International)

The Pulitzer Trophy—
1923

This was the fourth running of the Pulitzer series and by far the most successful and best-organized air race yet held in the United States. The city of St. Louis turned itself inside out to make the 1923 International Air Races (as they were called this year) an enduring testament as to how air races should be organized. Bridges were built, roads widened—even the airport itself was enlarged—and general spectator amenities were much improved over any American air races to date.

This year's Mitchell and Pulitzer races were the last events in a series of nine, held in beautiful weather October 4 and 6. Originally slated for October 1 and 3, the races were postponed after heavy rains on September 30 flooded St. Louis Field.

The rivalry for the Mitchell Trophy was particularly fierce this year. It had been decided that the winner should not only receive an impressive piece of hardware, he would also win the opportunity to fly the Army's entry in the following year's Pulitzer! As all six entrants were to fly identical Thomas-Morse MB-3's (chosen by lot just before the race), this would clear up any internecine disagreements within the 1st Pursuit Group.

At one o'clock the MB-3's were lined up and the pilots climbed aboard. Lieutenant T. W. Blackburn was first away on the four laps of the Pulitzer circuit. He was followed at thirty-second intervals by Lieutenant T. K. Mathews, Lieutenant C. P. Tourtellot, Captain V. B. Dixon, Lieutenant J. T. Johnson, and Captain Burt E. Skeel. Skeel also happened to be the C.O. of the 1st Pursuit Group, and it was quite obvious why as soon as he got off the ground. He put up the fastest lap, and ran off with the race as well, finishing with an average of 161 m.p.h. Only Mathews experienced mechanical trouble, fuel feed problems forcing him down at the end of his third lap.

For a time it appeared there would be some foreign Pulitzer competition for the Americans to meet. L. L. Carter of England had announced his intention of entering a modified Gloster-Napier. Unfortunately this challenge came to naught as Carter was unable to effect the necessary modifications to his ship to get its landing speed down below the Pulitzer's regulation 75 m.p.h. Also, Italian ace Brack-Papa and flyer-engineer Mario Fossati had both entered Fiat biplanes powered by colossal 800 h.p. V-12s. Equally regrettably these two entries did not complete either, but this was the first hint of some startling surprises in store for American pilots.

On race day of the Pulitzer, the sixth of October, the list of entries stood as follows:

First Lieutenant Lawson H. Saunderson	Wright TX	U.S.M.C.
First Lieutenant John D. Corkill	Army-Curtiss R-6	U.S.A.
Ensign Alford J. Williams	Curtiss R2C-1	U.S.N.
First Lieutenant Alexander Pearson	Verville-Sperry	U.S.A.
First Lieutenant Stephen W. Callaway	Wright TX	U.S.N.
First Lieutenant Harold J. Brow	Curtiss R2C-1	U.S.N.
First Lieutenant Walter Miller	Army-Curtiss R-6	U.S.A.

Something like one hundred thousand people turned out to watch this Pulitzer. They were not to be disappointed as, again, a fresh set of world records were established before their very eyes.

Again, the race was run in three heats, this time of two, two, and three aircraft. At about two-fifteen the starter gave the stand-by signal to the first two aircraft, and a few moments later the "go" signal followed. Lieutenant Lawson Saunderson lifted his roaring, 700 h.p., blood-red Navy-Wright racer off the runway, seemed almost immediately to reach four thousand feet, rolled over, dived toward the starting line, and slammed past it at something over 250 m.p.h. Lieutenant Corkill followed immediately in the 1922 Army-Curtiss racer, made his dive from about three thousand feet, and the race was on.

Saunderson began swallowing each thirty-mile lap in a little over eight minutes, averaging around 230 m.p.h. Poor Corkill was flying the only Curtiss aircraft in the race that hadn't been fitted with the new CD-12-A engine (it was virtually unchanged, except for the propeller, from its original 1922 form). He was giving away about 235 h.p. to Saunderson, and it showed in his lap times. He could do no better than 210–215 m.p.h. per lap. So it was at the finish of the first heat, with Saunderson recording a race average of 230.06 m.p.h. and Corkill 216.45 m.p.h. Saunderson had his share of bad luck too, having to dump his Navy-Wright in a haystack a few moments after his last lap due to fuel feed problems. He luckily escaped with bumps and cuts.

The second heat rapidly became the personal property of Al Williams' Curtiss R2C-1. He not only ran off with the second heat, but also with the fourth Pulitzer as well, giving everyone present a demonstration in high-speed precision. Apart from his first tour (a little faster through diving onto the course), his fastest and slowest laps differed by only a quarter of a mile per hour.

Pearson, whose Verville-Sperry had followed Williams, had to turn back on his first lap with propeller problems. This left Williams up there by himself, but not for long. The Contest Committee decided to launch the third and last heat. Callaway, Brow, and Miller were off almost immediately, but none of them could catch Williams. Brow came closest with laps around 242 m.p.h., but even such a speed as this wasn't enough. When the smoke had cleared, the final placings stood as follows:

1st	Williams	Curtiss R2C-1	243.67 m.p.h.
2nd	Brow	Curtiss R2C-1	241.78 m.p.h.
3rd	Saunderson	Navy-Wright	230.06 m.p.h.
4th	Callaway	Navy-Wright	230.00 m.p.h.
5th	Miller	Army-Curtiss	218.00 m.p.h.
6th	Corkill	Army-Curtiss	216.45 m.p.h.

Army Lieutenant Walter Miller's R-6 storms across the field at St. Louis and into the 1923 Pulitzer Trophy race. Curtiss racers, to no one's surprise, took the first four places. (Smithsonian Institution)

Al Williams taxis back to the hangar after setting up a new world speed record of 266.6 m.p.h. (UPI)

A month later, on November 2 and 4, Williams and Brow took their R2C-1's up over Mitchel Field, Long Island. After an exhibition of hair-raising but "friendly" rivalry—during which both succeeded in breaking the world speed record several times—they finally retired after Williams had shoved the new high up to 266.6 m.p.h. On December 11 the following year Adj. Bonnet in a Bernard-Ferbois finally took Williams' record at 278.48 m.p.h.

Immediately after this fourth Pulitzer, Williams admitted that he had been beset by strange reactions during his flight. "Somewhere in the third lap I went woozy. I felt just like I was asleep. It was those turns that did it." Indeed it was. And the same thing had bothered Maughan back in '22. Although the principle was fairly well understood by many, even in 1923, a new and highly unnerving experience was soon to become an everyday part of the racing pilot's experience: Blackout.

The Pulitzer Trophy— 1924

This year's Mitchell Trophy qualifier for the following year's Pulitzer was a more or less open-and-shut case for once, due mainly to the appearance of one of the finest pilots ever to fly for the United States air forces. Shortly after 1 P.M. on October 2 the eleven P-W-8's were lined up, and the pilots were told which aircraft they were to fly. As soon as they were aboard and started up they were given the starting signal at ten-second intervals.

The story of the race need occupy no more than three words: Lieutenant Cyrus Bettis. The way he cut and thrust his way around the course was masterful. He won at an average of 175 m.p.h. and put an end once more to barracks-room disagreements, at least for a while. More would be heard from Bettis.

Only four aircraft were to contest the Pulitzer this year, held at Dayton, Ohio, on October 4. Captain Burt Skeel (last year's Mitchell Trophy winner) and Lieutenant Wendell Brookley were to fly the two Curtiss racers. These aircraft were somewhat dated now, but nonetheless one of them was an almost certain winner. Lieutenant H. H. Mills was to fly the Verville-Sperry which had been built for the 1922 Pulitzer. It now had its Hisso replaced by a Curtiss CD-12 and was fitted with wing radiators instead of the original Lamblin-type. Rex Stoner was to fly a more or less standard P-W-8 fitted with a special Curtiss engine which was presently under test.

At two-fifteen two bombs were fired from the timer's stand and Skeel and Brookley tore off the runway and began their climb before diving over the starting line. Skeel reached three thousand feet, rolled over, and began his descent. As he

Lineup for the 1924 Pulitzer race. Left to right: Skeel, Brookley, Mills and Stoner.

reached one thousand feet, his upper wingtips suddenly ripped away, and then as the crowd watched, frozen, his entire aircraft seemed to tear apart as it streaked downward. Completely helpless, the roar of his engine suddenly silent, Skeel smashed into the ground at over 300 m.p.h.

Brookley, who had been following Skeel down, had to break his dive to avoid the trail of debris left by Skeel's disintegrating aircraft. No one knew better than Brookley that he was flying an airframe virtually identical to Skeel's, yet with a nerve-wracking display of raw guts, he dived again from two thousand feet, flashed over the start and onto the course.

Stoner and Mills were under way by now, but any interest in the outcome of the race had dissolved with Skeel's terrible accident (later shown to be the result of a thrown propeller blade).

For the record, Mills won the 1924 Pulitzer Trophy with his Verville-Sperry at 216.72 m.p.h., a surprising turn of speed for this aircraft. Brookley was second at 214.45 m.p.h., obviously holding back to keep his Curtiss in one piece.

Stoner was third at 168 m.p.h. They won five thousand, twenty-five hundred, and fifteen hundred dollars respectively in Government bonds.

As a result of Skeel's death, a serious re-examination of structural design and maintenance procedures was undertaken throughout the Air Service. Only a short while before, Lieutenant Alexander Pearson had been killed in a Curtiss racer, through wing collapse, while on a test flight for this Pulitzer. Nevertheless, this kind of thing was to happen again and again now, and many brave and gifted men would give their lives before a rigid system of aircraft maintenance and inspection procedures were adopted by the services.

The Pulitzer Trophy—
1925

This year's air races were held at Mitchel Field, Long Island, October 8–13. The Mitchell Trophy was contested over ten laps of a twelve-mile course, and was flown by ten of the 1st Pursuit Group's top pilots, all flying P-W-8's again. As the course had been shortened considerably, the lap speeds were somewhat lower than those of the previous year.

Lieutenant T. K. Mathews was declared the winner of this year's Mitchell Trophy race, which he led all the way. Mathews' speed for the course averaged 161.7 m.p.h.

This year's Pulitzer (it was to be the last) was run over four laps of a 31.07-mile course, and was split into two heats of two and four aircraft, possibly to add a little interest as there were really only two aircraft in the race: Al Williams' Curtiss Navy Racer and Cyrus Bettis' new Curtiss Army Racer—both bigger, heavier, and considerably stronger than previous Curtiss racing aircraft.

These new Curtiss R3C-1 racers were also a good deal faster. Williams had recently had his well over 300 m.p.h. in tests with an advanced new Curtiss engine, but the combination wasn't deemed reliable enough for the race. Both aircraft were now fitted with the new, but more familiar 620 h.p. Curtiss V-1400.

It was a cold and gusty afternoon when the aircraft were at last moved to the starting area and the mechanics began running up the engines. The second heat was also ready, and was comprised of Navy Lieutenants Cuddihy and Norton in standard Curtiss pursuits, and a P-W-8 and P-1 to be flown by

Cyrus Bettis whips past the finishing pylon, sewing up the last race for the Pulitzer Trophy with an average of 248.99 m.p.h. Bettis died following an air crash only a few months later. (Smithsonian Institution)

Captain H. W. Cook and Lieutenant L. H. Dawson, respectively.

Williams had won the toss-up and was first away, followed two minutes later by Bettis. After flying around the field for a few minutes to warm up, Williams shot past the start at such a rate that the fabric "streamline" cover over one of his wheels tore away. Fortunately, this was all that came loose and he steamed off down the course, looking very much like a winner.

Cyrus Bettis had other ideas, however. After his two-minute wait he was off and running, and it was very clear that the contest was far from decided. Both succeeded in beating Williams' old closed-course record of 243.67 m.p.h. on their first laps. Bettis' second lap was over 248 m.p.h., and his third over 249 m.p.h. Much to Williams' (and the Navy's) annoyance, his engine started to go sour and he began dropping back after his first lap, so Bettis came home the winner with a race average of 248.99 m.p.h.

The second heat now sedately made their way around the course, Army Lieutenant Dawson taking the honors for this one at 169.9 m.p.h., with Cuddihy retiring on his last lap.

All in all, it had been a great day for the Army (once again the Navy was nowhere this year), with much back-slapping and hat-tossing. As one of Bettis' mechanics beamed afterward, "Tonight we eat pie!"

Bettis being congratulated after his win. (UPI)

The Schneider Trophy— 1925

The Schneider race which was to have been held on October 25, 1924, was canceled by the Americans three weeks before race day. What with the withdrawal of the Italian entries and assorted troubles in the English camp, the Flying Club of Baltimore quite sportingly decided not to hold the contest. (Biard's aircraft wasn't ready in time, and Broad's Gloster-Napier sank after a trial flight.) A sort of aerial regatta was held instead, and a great success it was too. Lieutenant George Cuddihy, flying the previous year's winning Curtiss CR-3, set up a string of new world records for seaplanes, with one run over the three kilometers at 188.1 m.p.h.

Al Williams' Pulitzer-winning R2C-1 of 1923 had been fitted with floats and recently timed, unofficially, at just under 230 m.p.h. David Rittenhouse was the pilot during these runs. It didn't appear at Baltimore, however, the Navy sneakily deciding to keep it under wraps until the following year's race.

On Saturday, September 26, 1925, the good ship *Minnewaska* sailed from London for Baltimore, Maryland, bearing the hopes of the British aviation industry, and one of the most beautiful machines ever crafted by the hand of man: the Supermarine S-4, designed by R. J. Mitchell.

The S-4 was more than beautiful. A few days before the *Minnewaska* sailed, the S-4 had slammed through the traps over Southampton Water at 226.752 m.p.h., shattering Cuddihy's seaplane record, and at only about three-quarters throttle! Surely, Britain's Schneider chances hadn't looked so good since Pixton had clobbered all opposition in 1914, or since that debacle in 1919.

The British were also sending over two new Gloster-Napier III biplanes, to be flown by Hubert Broad and Bert Hinkler. Even without the S-4 the British team would have been pretty well set up this year, Broad also having flown one of the new Glosters at a speed well over Cuddihy's old mark.

About three weeks before race day the Italian team, with pilots Giovanni de Briganti and Ricardo Morselli, began to arrive. They were immaculate and slickly organized—but they were also hopelessly outclassed. Their Macchi M-33 flying boats (with Curtiss D-12 engines!) were the fastest of their type in the world, but the days of the flying boat as a pure speed machine were gone. Certainly the Italians knew this, but they came anyway, simply out of their love of competition, and their desire to learn. How well they learned would be startlingly clear a year later.

The American team was to be represented by Navy Lieutenants George Cuddihy and Ralph Ofstie, who were to fly the new Curtiss R3C-2 racers, with Lieutenant Frank Conant's R2C-2 (Al Williams' 1923 Pulitzer winner) in reserve. And

Supermarine designer R. J. Mitchell's breathtakingly beautiful S-4 shortly after its completion. Even before this aircraft arrived at Baltimore, it had already shattered Cuddihy's old seaplane speed record, and looked very much like a winner. (Central News Ltd.)

One of the two Macchi M-33 flying boats brought over by the Italian team. (Smithsonian Institution)

A dramatic shot of Doolittle in a vertical bank as he whipped around the home pylon. (UPI)

for the first time, the U.S. Army was to make a bid for the Schneider Trophy. Cyrus Bettis' 1925 Pulitzer winner had been fitted with floats during the intervening twelve days, and had shown a maximum in trials of only about 15 m.p.h. less than it had as a landplane. To this already remarkable aircraft, now designated R3C-2, the Army now added their own secret weapon. It was called Lieutenant Jimmy Doolittle.

As the foreign entries arrived at Baltimore, their aircraft were sheltered in rather makeshift tent-hangars which were later a source of considerable irritation to some of the competitors. During a gale which blew up without warning a few days before race day (and which resulted in a postponement till the following week), the crews had quite a job keeping the shelters from collapsing onto the aircraft. Biard's S-4 received a falling tent pole on its tail and a fair amount of damage as a result, but it was repaired in time for the beginning of the trials.

On the morning of October 23 the seaworthiness ordeal was begun, and almost immediately heartbreaking disappointment struck the British team. Biard, in his last test flight with the S-4, was whipping his aircraft through a series of fast, sharp turns when he suddenly found himself fighting violent wing flutter. Unable to regain control, he hit the water more or less right side up, the impact tearing off the floats. The aircraft sank immediately—with the stunned Biard tightly strapped to his seat with a broken wrist. Moments later Biard was partially buried in mud at the bottom of Chesapeake Bay. The icy water quickly brought him around and, struggling with only one hand, he at last managed to free himself and get to the surface. Then he literally almost froze to death before the rescue launch found him. Biard was well on the mend within a few days, but the exquisite S-4 was completely, and permanently, destroyed.

During the remainder of the trials all other entrants got through without incident—except for Bert Hinkler. Due to bad weather he didn't get a chance to undergo the trials until the morning of the race. The swell was much too heavy when he went out, and it was only a matter of minutes before the struts on the undercarriage of his aircraft collapsed. Now Broad was the only British entry left.

Biard's S-4 was to have been the first over the speed course.

Biard moves off into what was to become the S-4's last flight. (UPI)

All that remained of Biard's Supermarine after his accident. (UPI)

Doolittle took his place, and was first away at 2:38 P.M. The rest of the competitors followed Doolittle at five-minute intervals, but they needn't have bothered. From the moment he got onto the course it was obvious that nothing could catch him. The U.S. Army romped away with the race, toppling world

Hubert Broad looking over his Gloster-Napier III biplane. Broad flew this aircraft to a very creditable second place. (UPI)

Broad "on the step" during the taxiing trials. (UPI)

closed-course records on every lap, and averaging 232.573 m.p.h. for the distance.

If Doolittle hadn't been there, Britain would have won the Schneider Trophy anyway with Hubert Broad's very creditable second place at 199.169 m.p.h., this speed also breaking the former world record for seaplanes. De Briganti was third at 168.44 m.p.h. This Italian, incidentally, along with Doolittle, gave everyone present an extremely impressive demonstration of how to get around corners in a hurry.

Cuddihy's engine ran out of oil a mile from the finish, immediately overheated, and burst into flame. He promptly put it out with a small fire extinguisher, but forfeited a certain second place.

To drive the point home, Doolittle set a new outright world speed record for seaplanes shortly after the race, averaging 245.713 m.p.h. in three passes over the three kilometers. For the second time America had won the Schneider Trophy, and in no uncertain fashion. The chances were now better than even that the United States could win it outright within the next three years.

For the British, and the Italians, it was now or never.

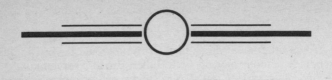

The Schneider Trophy— 1926

The ninth Schneider contest was held on the eleventh through the thirteenth of November 1926, in perfect weather (after three postponements).

England did not compete this year. Rumor had it that the Air Ministry, after dawdling about until the end of 1925, had placed orders for three aircraft to compete the following year. But the Schneider had by now become an extremely complicated business; one could no longer throw an aircraft together in a few months and expect it to win. The English, already too late, were now aiming at 1927, and the Italians had already begun construction of their 1926 Schneider entries almost a year before. The Americans were going to field the previous year's winner, but they might as well have sent up butterflies.

When the Italian team arrived at Norfolk, the Americans were absolutely stunned at their progress over the intervening year. In the United States the silly argument as to which was potentially faster, biplanes or monoplanes, was still soberly discussed into the small hours. The Italians presented three sleek Macchi 39 monoplanes with the cleanest frontal aspect of any aircraft yet seen anywhere (except perhaps for the Supermarine S-4), and their engines developed at least 100 horsepower more than the most powerful American entry. For the Yanks, the writing was on the wall.

Strangely enough, the Italians knew little more about their new aircraft than anyone else did. Very little testing had been carried out, and one of them had already killed the Italian Marchese Centurione on a test flight. This did not add to their peace of mind.

Major Mario de Bernardi, and the Macchi M-39, the winning combination in 1926. (Smithsonian Institution)

The American team had also recently suffered a serious loss. Lieutenant Frank Conant, U.S.N., who was to have captained the United States team, was killed only ten days before on his way to Norfolk in a U.S. Navy seaplane.

On the day of the trials, the entries stood as follows:

Italy	Major Mario de Bernardi, team captain	Macchi M-39
	Captain Arturo Ferrarin	Macchi M-39
	Lieutenant Adriano Bacula	Macchi M-39
	Captain Guascone Guasconi, reserve	
U.S.A.	Pilot for Conant's aircraft not yet announced	Curtiss R3C-4
	Lieutenant Christian Schilt, U.S.M.C.	Curtiss R3C-2
	Lieutenant George Cuddihy, U.S.N.	Curtiss R3C-3

Late on Thursday afternoon, the eleventh, the trials were begun by Major de Bernardi who completed his tests without a hitch—well, almost. As he was waiting to be brought in after finishing his starboard pontoon was stupidly rammed by a tow launch trying to hook up. Fortunately his aircraft was brought up the slipway before it was too late, and it was agreed he could undergo the mooring test the following day after repairs.

De Bernardi's M-39 being brought up the slipway after the speed trials. (Smithsonian Institution)

Next, Lieutenant Schilt took his R3C-2 out, shortly followed by Lieutenant Bacula, both of whom completed their trials successfully.

Then, though the light by now was fading fast, Captain Ferrarin went out, completed the first half of his trials, and then—just disappeared! A motor launch was sent out to find him, which was shortly followed by a Navy flying boat. It was now quite dark, yet somehow the pilot of the flying boat spotted Ferrarin—drifting with a dead engine, without lights, in the middle of the heavy shipping channel at Hampton Roads. Luckily the tow launch found him before a freighter did.

On Friday morning there was still some confusion as to who would fill the gap left by the death of Lieutenant Conant. This was soon resolved when Lieutenant William G. Tomlinson, one of the reserve Navy pilots, climbed aboard the R3C-3 (which really should have been flown by Cuddihy) and began checking it out for the trials.

Due to his lack of familiarity with his mount, Tomlinson's takeoff on his trials was very ragged. What with its reversed propeller rotation, due to the geared Packard engine, and numerous trim peculiarities, this was a very difficult aircraft to manage. Once airborne, however, Tomlinson handled it perfectly—until the time came to put it down again. He was forced to break his first approach to avoid another aircraft. On his second he leveled off too early, stalled about two or three feet above the water, bounced, skidded, flipped over, sank and settled with just the bottoms of the Curtiss' pontoons showing above the surface of the water. Exit what was thought to be the fastest American entry. Tomlinson fortunately suffered nothing more than a "severe ducking." Later in the day he qualified a ridiculously outclassed Curtiss F6C-2 for the following day's race, though one wonders why.

Cuddihy had meanwhile completed the trials in Conant's R3C-4.

It still promised to be a very close race. Educated guesses by the Americans estimated the Italian lap speeds would be in the 230's. Conant had flown the R3C-4 at a carefully observed, though unofficial, 256 m.p.h. a few days before, and Admiral Moffett (Chief of the Bureau of Aeronautics) was assuring everyone that the R3C-3 had once hit 258 m.p.h., though it hardly mattered now. The Italians weren't saying anything, but they were smiling . . .

By Saturday morning, the roads leading into Norfolk and Newport News were jammed solid with cars trying to get near the course. About thirty thousand did. The news media, both local and national, had played up this event for all it was worth,

Tomlinson's R3C-3 on the way to the trials. He came back without his aircraft. (Smithsonian Institution)

and the public's response was overwhelming. Would the Americans win the Schneider Trophy permanently? Would they lose it back to the Europeans? They were soon to find out as a combined four-thousand horsepower began warming up for the speed trials.

Shortly after two-thirty, Lieutenant Bacula's M-39 was lowered down the slipway. In less than a minute he was airborne and tearing off down the course. Five minutes later Tomlinson was sent off. Then Cuddihy left in place of Ferrarin, whose engine was not running well at the start (he followed Cuddihy one minute later).

Bacula's first lap was covered at a surprisingly low 209 m.p.h., and American hopes perked up considerably at this. Tomlinson on the other hand was picking his way around the course at 137 m.p.h.

Suddenly, Cuddihy came through ending his first lap at 232.427 m.p.h.! And immediately, through the cheers, it was announced that Ferrarin's first lap had beaten Cuddihy's time by a scant 2 m.p.h. The enormous crowd was cheering wildly with every announcement over the public address system.

By this time Major de Bernardi had taken off, followed a minute later by Schilt in the previous year's winner. Shortly afterward Cuddihy came by again, barely beating Ferrarin's time, only to be beaten *again* by him by 2 m.p.h.! After this lap Ferrarin retired with dropping oil pressure, leaving De Bernardi to carry on for Italy—Bacula was now too far behind to be in contention.

De Bernardi's first 239 m.p.h. lap was the fastest one yet—but it was also his slowest. He cut all the next six laps about ten miles per hour faster, and obviously had plenty in hand. Schilt tried his best, but his Curtiss just simply wasn't fast enough.

Cuddihy had to retire on his last lap with a failing fuel transfer pump, and Tomlinson was nowhere. The finishing averages were:

De Bernardi	246.5 m.p.h.
Schilt	231.4 m.p.h.
Bacula	218.7 m.p.h.
Tomlinson	136.7 m.p.h.

George Cuddihy's R3C-4 is lowered down the slipway a few minutes before the start of the Schneider race. He was forced to retire with fuel feed problems on his last lap. (Smithsonian Institution)

Marine Lieutenant Christian Schilt about to start up his R3C-2. Schilt was awarded the Medal of Honor two years later during the Nicaraguan campaign. (UPI)

The Italians won this Schneider for three simple reasons: their aircraft were miles ahead aerodynamically, their engines were vastly more powerful, and pilots just didn't come any better.

So America lost her chance for permanent possession of the Schneider Trophy through falling asleep at the switch. It was almost a pleasure though to hand it over to the Italians. They had all been so charming, so cooperative, so modest . . . and so bloody fast.

The Schneider Trophy— 1927

During the summer of 1927 Britain finally got her High-Speed Flight, a hand-picked group of the R.A.F.'s finest pilots, who would represent her in the Schneider series. British aviation journalists had been clamoring for just such an arrangement for years, and perhaps the all too obvious success of a similar organization demonstrated the year before by the Italians at Norfolk had helped things along.

The United States Government was now pretending that the Schneider contests had ceased to exist, so any efforts made by the U.S.A. would of necessity be private ones. As a result America would never possess the Schneider Trophy again, but more importantly, it would take about fifteen years for American technicians to learn lessons that the British and Italians learned in 1927. It would be even longer before the United States again possessed the world's fastest aircraft. Such is the high cost of economizing.

By mid-August it had been announced that Britain, Italy, and the U.S.A. would compete for the Trophy, and that the contest would be held off the Lido beach, outside Venice, on the twenty-third and twenty-fourth of September. By this time rumors had already been filtering through to England that the Fiat Company, which was preparing the power plants for the Macchi entries, had destroyed six engines during bench tests. Whether this meant that there were serious design faults or that they were simply pushing them over the limit to detect and correct possible weaknesses, remained to be seen. The British were certainly taking this Schneider seriously. Seven aircraft, built solely for this event, were under test. Three from Supermarine, three from the Gloster firm—all powered by the magnificent Napier "Lion," and one from Short Brothers, the famous flying boat constructors, powered by a radial Bristol "Mercury" engine.

In the United States, Al Williams, a perfectly-cast Schneider pilot if there ever was one, had announced that he would enter a 1250 h.p. Packard-powered biplane built by the Kirkham Products Corporation. This aircraft had been designed to bring the air-speed record back to the U.S.A. and had been under construction for nearly a year. After it had been fitted with floats, Williams was constantly dogged by bad weather, only managing four flights in it over several weeks. Eventually, after running out of time for shakedown flights, Williams was forced to announce his withdrawal on September 9.

The first members of the British contingent arrived in Venice on August 30, Squadron Leader L. H. Slatter and Flight Lieutenant O. E. Worsley being welcomed enthusiastically by the Italian officials. The next day three of the aircraft arrived aboard the S.S. *Eworth,* and the work of unloading, unpacking, and assembly was begun. Unfortunately bad weather prevented any attempt at test flights for ten days after their arrival. By this

Al Williams aboard the Kirkham-Packard biplane which was eventually withdrawn. (UPI)

time the rest of the aircraft had arrived, as well as the remainder of the High-Speed Flight: Flight Lieutenants S. M. Kinkead and S. N. Webster, and Flying Officer H. M. Schofield. On the tenth the first test flights were made, Slatter taking up S-5 N-222 for an exploratory spin around the course. Then Kinkead took the Gloster-Napier IV-B out for a trial run and succeeded in frightening the daylights out of the bathers along the Lido beach with a few ground-level bursts at around 300 m.p.h.

It wasn't only the bathers who were impressed. Unknown to the British, the Italians were having maddening engine problems. Their Fiat AS-3 engines, originally designed to produce 550–590 h.p., were now belting out over 970 h.p., and the Italians were fighting a losing battle to keep them from flying apart. To cap it all off, they had timed Slatter's S-5 during his trial flight at 312 m.p.h., a much better speed than their Macchis could equal if they were to last the distance.

The Italian team was to field three Macchi M-52 monoplanes. They would be flown by the familiar Captain Arturo Ferrarin, Major Mario de Bernardi (who had won the Schneider Trophy for Italy the previous year), and Captain Feder Guazetti, a top pilot of the Regia Aeronautica.

During the test flights of the succeeding days, one incident occurred which might be mentioned. Flying Officer Schofield took the Short-Bristol "Crusader" out for a trial flight on Sunday the eleventh. No sooner had he lifted off the water when he did a jerky half-roll and slammed back into the sea again. The impact tore the aircraft to bits and ripped off most of Schofield's clothing, smashing his goggles against his forehead. Bewildered, half-drowned, and infuriated, he was carried off to the nearby Italian Naval Hospital. When his aircraft had been reclaimed, it was found that the aileron control cables had been reversed! The best-laid plans . . .

By Friday the twenty-third, the day of the navigability trials, the pilots and aircraft which would represent Great Britain had been selected. Kinkead would fly the Gloster-Napier IV-B with the geared propeller, and Webster and Worsley two of the three S-5's, Webster's propeller also being slightly geared down.

All aircraft completed their trials without mishap, except for Webster, who was caught by an unexpected gust of wind during his taxiing test and suddenly found himself airborne.

The three Macchi M-52's at the start of the mooring test. Kinkead's aircraft can be seen at far left. (Flight International)

Shortly after all the aircraft had been moored for the six-hour water-tightness tests, the skies opened up and a torrent of rain, followed by hail, descended upon them. One can only attempt to imagine the thoughts running through the minds of the teams as they watched hail-stones the size of golf balls bouncing off the delicate wing radiators . . . However, after the mooring tests were completed no apparent damage had befallen any of the aircraft, and they were put away for the following day's race, but the weather was looking none too promising.

By Saturday morning it was clear that there could be no speed trials that day. However, it had taken the Commissaires Sportives an entire day to make up their minds about Webster's accidental flight during his taxiing test. They now required him to go through it again, and he did, this time faultlessly. A postponement of the speed trials until the following Monday had also been declared, and the two teams settled down to wait the last few hours and consider their chances.

Monday turned out to be an excellent day, although somewhat overcast, and though there was still a moderate swell to the sea, neither of these factors would present much of a problem. At 11 A.M. it was announced that the race would begin at two-thirty that afternoon.

At one-forty the public address system announced that all aircraft had left their hangars and were on their way to the course. By this time an unbelievable crowd of over two hundred thousand had turned up and were packed like sardines the entire length of the Lido.

Promptly at two-thirty it was announced that Kinkead had received his starting signal; at two-thirty-two he thundered past the start about thirty feet above the beach, and almost at once

Kinkead takes out in M-221 for her maiden flight. (National Archives)

Flight Lieutenant S. N. Webster tries out one of the brand new supermarine S-5's at Calshot. Once again, R. J. Mitchell had surpassed himself in designing the S-5. (Smithsonian Institution)

Side view of the Gloster-Napier IV-B, surely the most beautiful, and certainly the fastest, biplane ever built. (Smithsonian Institution)

became a speck on the horizon. Next past was De Bernardi, flying somewhat higher and not apparently as fast as Kinkead, though his engine seemed to be running well. After Kinkead came past, ending his first lap, Webster's S-5 took off and flashed past the line at two-forty-three.

As Webster crossed the start-finish line De Bernardi arrived again, ending his first lap. The Italians had developed a rather spectacular method of coping with these almost 180-degree turns—a sort of half-loop followed by a half roll . . . almost an Immelmann, but done at a slight angle to get around the pylon. It was a breathtaking maneuver to watch, but its efficiency was held in some doubt by the British team who had tried it back at Calshot and found it slightly slower than the flat, wide turns they were now using.

Turns notwithstanding, as they flew by together it was suddenly very clear to the spectators that Webster's aircraft was considerably faster than De Bernardi's.

Next away was Guazetti, at two-fifty-three. It was later known that the Italians had suffered such engine troubles with the AS-3's that Guazetti's aircraft had been fitted with the winning AS-2 engine of the previous year. It wasn't enough.

Then followed Worsley in S-5 N-219, and his engine seemed to have a sharper edge than the other Napiers. Then suddenly word came through that De Bernardi was down. He had been eliminated by lubrication problems leading to engine seizure, but this was only the beginning of the Italian's bad luck. . . .

Ferrarin's Macchi had shot past the start, running quite roughly, and was forced to retire from the race while still on his first lap. Scratch another AS-3. During all this time Kinkead, Webster, and Worsley were going around like trains, Kinkead setting the pace with laps around 280 m.p.h. Their regularity was broken though when Kinkead had to slow up due to violent engine vibration caused by a suddenly unbalanced spinner. On his sixth lap he just managed to put down, completely covered in hot oil, before the front of the aircraft was shaken apart.

Then the Italians' last hope, Guazetti, was blinded by a sudden fuel leak while hanging on his prop in one of his 180-degree turns. He miraculously managed to put down again without incident.

Webster and Worsley went on to finish in that order, and win the Schneider Trophy once more for Britain. Their finishing times were: Webster, 281.669 m.p.h.; Worsley, 273.088 m.p.h. Webster's *average* for the course had exceeded the world's speed record held by Adj. Bonnet.

The British Schneider Trophy racers were now the fastest aircraft in the world.

The unfortunate retirement of all the Italian entries from this event was surely lamented by all right-thinking Italians, for this was surely a body blow to their national prestige. De Bernardi recouped a lot of it, though, on November 4 when

De Bernardi flashes past the start on his opening lap. (Flight International)

Guazetti in one of his spectacular, but not very effective, turns. (Flight International)

he set up a new world record of speed of 296.84 m.p.h. in one of the M-52's with a Fiat AS-3 that *was* running well!

On the afternoon of March 12 of the following year, Flight Lieutenant Kinkead took a specially tuned S-5 up over Southampton Water, intent on beating De Bernardi's record. (This was considered to be foregone, as he had been unofficially timed at over 330 m.p.h. the day before.) When he was about halfway through his first high-speed run through the traps his aircraft suddenly slammed into the water without any apparent reason or later explanation. He was killed instantly.

Eighteen days later, on March 30, De Bernardi was over the Lido again, and this time he boosted the new world speed record to 318.57 m.p.h. If only he could have had it running that way a few months before . . .

In December 1927 His Excellency General Italo Balbo, the Italian Under Secretary of State for Air, visited England to discuss with various officials there the possibility of holding the Schneider races every two years, fixing the date for the next contest for late 1929. As there seemed to be general agreement all around—from the U.S.A., France, and Germany—the resolution was adopted. Now there could be *no* excuses. . . .

Kinkead (below) and Webster charging along the Lido beach. Kinkead was consistently recording the fastest laps until he was forced down. (Flight International)

A view of part of the opening ceremonies at the 1929 Nationals in Cleveland. (Smithsonian Institution)

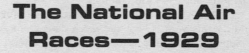

The National Air
Races—1929

By 1929 the National Air Races, particularly since the end of the Pulitzer contests, had degenerated into an annual aerial sideshow. Certainly the world's most exciting and elaborate sideshow, but a sideshow nonetheless. The great names were still there, along with many soon-to-be-great, and the flying was almost always flawless, but the aircraft were . . . well frankly, they were dull.

To most people, nothing of any importance seemed to have happened to aviation in the U.S.A. since 1925. They weren't too far wrong. The Europeans had now grabbed hold of the ball and had run off and hidden with it, while the U.S. Government was behaving as though there had never been any game to begin with.

General Billy Mitchell had tried every way he knew to force some semblance of life and reality into the awareness of those who were blocking the development of U.S. aeronautics. He was court-martialed for his trouble in December 1925. A band of ignorant, rigid old men had American aviation by the throat and seemed to be doing their best to stifle the life out of it.

Any advancements in design were now up to private interests alone, with more blunt lessons from the Europeans to keep them on their toes.

There's no denying that these early National Air Races were popular. About half a million people *paid* to see the 1929 show in Cleveland, August 27 through September 2, and huge crowds had also appeared at Philadelphia, Spokane, and Los Angeles from 1926 through 1928. This year at Cleveland, what began as just another aerial display ended by recharting many a designer's ideas about the direction he was headed in. It could almost have been written and produced by Walt Disney, as one quite simple aircraft from a young, aggressive company in Kansas succeeded in making the entire U.S. Navy and Army Air Corps look perfectly ridiculous.

It seems as though there was an event scheduled for anything that could fly this year. Over the seven days from August 27 through September 2 there were displays of balloon bursting, parachute jumping, acrobatics, and formation flying, as well as races for airplanes, gliders, blimps, and even pigeons. There were cross-country races and closed course races, men's events and women's events. But the most significant event of all, as we look back on it today, was the unlimited free-for-all race on Monday, September 2.

There were eleven entries in this race, but the chief interest was expected to lie in the contest between the two military service Curtiss aircraft flown by Army Lieutenant R. G. Breene, in a P-3-A, and Lieutenant Commander J. J. Clarke flying a U.S. Navy Hawk. As these were both front-line pursuit ships, and this was the first occasion since 1925 that these two services would fly against each other, it seemed highly unlikely that outsiders would occupy much of the limelight. Among the other entrants was a certain Roscoe Turner who would fly a Lockheed Vega, with which he had placed second in a race for closed-cabin aircraft earlier in the day, and a Mr. Douglas Davis who was to fly a brand-new Travel Air monoplane. This aircraft rapidly became known as the "Mystery Ship" because as soon as Davis arrived with it at Cleveland Airport he had it towed into a hangar, hidden by tarpaulins, and refused to answer any questions or let anybody look at it.

Spectators got a fleeting opportunity to see it on the day before the free-for-all race when Davis took it out for a final shakedown and a little mild stunting near the field. Davis almost gave the show away when he went into a vertical climb—and *stayed* there! Surprisingly, no one seemed to take much interest then, but everyone certainly did the next day.

This year the aircraft competing in the new closed-course Thompson Cup race were started at ten-second intervals, with their wheels on the starting line and fifty feet between wingtips. At the drop of the flag they were to take off and fly straight ahead to a scattering pylon, then return and get onto the course proper. From the spectator's viewpoint this was a much better arrangement than starting competitors off one by one with several minutes in between, as they could now know the position of each entry throughout the race. Naturally, this would also be a considerable aid to the pilots themselves.

It wasn't much help to them this year though. From the drop of the flag the race was clearly in Doug Davis' pocket. His little orange-and-black Travel Air "R" fairly leaped off the ground and the rest of the competitors hardly saw it again, except when it passed them, until the race was over, by which time they were wishing they had never seen it at all.

Davis completed the fifty-mile course in 14 minutes, 5.9 seconds, averaging 194.9 m.p.h. Breene was second at 186.8, then Turner at 163.4 and Clarke at 153.4. Davis' average would have been well over 200 m.p.h. if he hadn't missed a pylon on his second lap (his aircraft could do 235 m.p.h. easily). He had to turn back, get around the pylon, and then pass everybody again, *all in 50 miles!*

The American aviation press pounced on this episode and gleefully began rubbing the U.S. Government's nose in it. They demanded to know just how it came to pass that a commercial aircraft, freely available to anybody with the money to buy

Doug Davis' superb Travel Air "R," which sent both the Army and Navy back to the drawing boards after the race for the 1929 Thompson Cup. The design staff in Wichita was headed by Herb Rawdon, who later designed the famous "staggerwing" Beechcraft biplane. (Smithsonian Institution)

Doug Davis with the Thompson Cup. The Thompson Trophy was first offered the following year. (UPI)

one, could so easily outrun and outmaneuver the aircraft that were supposed to be protecting the United States from any and all aggressors.

It was a good question.

At least something seemed to be happening in United States aviation again. Maybe this was just the kick in the pants it needed. One thing was certain anyway: both the Army and the Navy would make damn sure they stayed out of any free-for-all races next year.

The Schneider Trophy—1929

On May 1, 1928, Jacques Schneider died at Beaulieu-sur-Mer, near Nice, where he had been staying for the last few months. He was only forty-nine and in considerably reduced circumstances, but he had received the immense satisfaction of watching the once rickety machines built in his name become the fastest, most advanced aircraft in the world.

After Kinkead's fatal accident in 1928, Great Britain's High-Speed Flight was reformed during the succeeding months. The new roster was comprised of Flight Lieutenants D'Arcy Greig and G. H. Stainforth, Flying Officers R. L. Atcherley, H. R. Waghorn, and T. H. Moon (who had served in 1927, as now, as Technical Officer). All of them (except Moon) had been flying instructors or examiners at Central Flying School.

On November 4 Greig took the Supermarine S-5 N-219 up in an official attempt to beat De Bernardi's latest record of 318.5 m.p.h. set seven months before, but he didn't make it. His four runs averaged 319.57 m.p.h., a shade faster all right, but not enough to be recognized by the F.A.I. (A full one percent increase was required.)

The following month it was announced that France, the United States, and Italy would compete with Great Britain for the Trophy. Also, the Dornier firm in Germany had expressed a desire to enter if sufficient backing, governmental or private, could be found to meet the cost of aircraft which was fully planned and ready to be built. Unfortunately nobody offered them the money.

By January 1929 the date of the contest had been fixed for

September 6 and 7, and Squadron Leader A. H. Orlebar, a priceless combination of brilliant test pilot *and* administrator, had been posted to Felixstowe to take command of the High-Speed Flight training program.

The race was to be held once more over the Solent, between the Isle of Wight and the English mainland. Also by this time, France, Italy, and the United States had announced their entries:

Sadi Lecointe, Fernand Lasne, Bonnet, and Demougeot comprised the announced team from France. Four aircraft were under construction: two Bernards and two Nieuport-Delage Type 650's (1000 h.p. Hissos). For Italy, De Bernardi, Ferrarin, Guazetti, and Guasconi were announced; and though there were a lot of rumors the Italians weren't saying anything officially about their entries. Al Williams of the United States was preparing a new racing seaplane built at the Naval Aircraft Factory in Philadelphia and designed by John Kean. It was also powered by the formidable Packard "X" engine which in its latest form was developing "something over 1550 h.p." Despite its promise it wasn't ready in time.

The British had built four aircraft this time. Two from Supermarine powered by a highly secret new Rolls-Royce "R" engine (which was putting out a whopping 1630 h.p., though only half a dozen people knew this), and two new ones from the Gloster concern which would be powered by what was surely the ultimate development of the amazing Napier "Lion"—its output was later known to be 1320 h.p., more than *four times* its originally designed limit.

By mid-August, the Italian Minister of Aeronautics had announced that the team of De Bernardi, Ferrarin, Guazetti, and Guasconi would step down in favor of a younger, and presumably quicker, group of pilots. They would be: Captain Giuseppe Motta, Lieutenants Giovanni Monti and Remo Cadringher, and non-coms Tomaso Dal Molin and Francesco Agello. Ironically, as the announcement was made, Motta, the Italians' best pilot, was killed while testing the brutal new Macchi M-67 over Lake Garda where the team's training operations were based. And during the previous month Agello had written off two of the tiny, but *very* fast Fiat C-29 racers—they had been forced to test in continuously bad weather. In desperation they tried for a month's postponement, but were refused. Once again the unlucky cards seemed to be stacking up against the Italians.

By this time the British team had moved to Calshot and had taken delivery of their first Rolls-Royce-powered S-6 (N-247), and as soon as its vices and unfamiliar habits had been felt out on the water, the first flights were made, with Orlebar at the controls (Orlebar carefully tested every aircraft himself before passing them on to the team). The appointed pilots were amazed at the speed of this machine—nearly 350 m.p.h. with the greatest of ease. A Gloster VI had also arrived, this time in a beautiful burnished-brass color. It was immediately dubbed the "Golden Arrow" by the press, though one journalist liked to call it the "bullet with a bow tie."

By now the Italian machines had also arrived at Calshot, and the British were enormously impressed with them. No less than six aircraft had been brought over: the one remaining Fiat C-29 racer, a very interesting twin-tandem-engined Savoia-Marchetti of a similar layout to the unbuilt Dornier entry, two

The extremely interesting Savoia-Marchetti S-65 with its twin-tandem engine configuration. Unfortunately, after it was built it was discovered that there was sufficient radiator area to permit only one engine to be run at a time. (Smithsonian Institution)

awesomely formidable Macchi M-67's, and two of the Macchi M-52's that had raced in 1927. One of these last was called the "Moor of Venice" because its once brilliant red paintwork had now degenerated to a grimy black through over four hundred hours as a flying testbed.

The weather didn't cooperate in England either, and precious days were lost waiting for the right combination of sea, wind, and visibility.

Both teams had discovered that their newer models were very difficult to get off the water with anything like a full load of fuel. This was mainly due to the vast increase in propeller torque, plus the fact that the new aircraft were so much heavier (the S-6 weighed 5325 pounds wet, and S-5 about 3200). The Glosters were least affected this way but they were plagued with fuel feed problems that would eventually keep them out of the race. The S-6's had to settle for a propeller with a flatter pitch to make quite sure they would be able to get off, though this would seriously aggravate what was already becoming a critical overheating problem. Now, to last the distance, the British entries would have to fly the race well under full throttle! (The Gloster company had developed a variable-pitch propeller back in 1925, but after a few successful test flights the idea was abandoned!)

During the following days both teams tried to successfully deal with their daily crises as their moment of truth loomed nearer. Remarkably, their routine was undisturbed by an endless succession of visits by inquisitive notables (the Prince of Wales was much in evidence, as was Lawrence of Arabia, now in his guise of "Aircraftsman Shaw").

At 9:15 A.M. on Friday, September 6, the trials were begun. Waghorn was first away in the S-6 (it was his birthday!) into an unpleasantly choppy sea, though the weather was beautiful. After quite a rough ride he completed his trials successfully. He was followed by Dal Molin, who also went through the trials faultlessly. Then Atcherley and Greig, also without incident. Monti's M-67 gave him a lot of trouble getting off, due to some confusion about wind direction, but his troubles had only begun. As he was alighting again, at about 130 m.p.h., he narrowly averted being killed due to the clumsiness of the battleship H.M.S. *Iron Duke,* which had chosen this moment to bungle its way onto the course, and into Monti's

The very fast, but unpredictable, Fiat C-29. Though three aircraft had been built, two were destroyed before the Italian team arrived at Calshot. Engine problems eliminated this one, too. (Smithsonian Institution)

way (Monti actually managed to joke about it afterward). Despite this interference Monti was able to complete his trials successfully, as did Cadringher, and the six-hour tie-up for the mooring test was begun.

Several hours had passed before Orlebar first noticed that Atcherley's S-6 N-248 was sinking! There was a decided list— and it was getting worse. Hurried calculations were made on the apparent rate of descent and it was found to be just about three hours before the aircraft would keel over. They couldn't touch it of course, so they spent the next 180 minutes or so holding their breath. They got it out just in time.

That midnight, as the finishing touches were being put to the British entries, one of the mechanics was removing the spark plugs from Waghorn's N-247. He saw something strange on one of them. It was a little silver speck, and he showed it to Moon, who almost had heart-failure. A piston was disintegrating! It would be quite impossible to describe the panic that reigned for the next six hours. It's enough to say that by 6:15 A.M. a new cylinder block and piston had been fitted, and all present were nervous, and physical, wrecks. This little

The Macchi M-52 "Moor of Venice" which had served the Italian team so well. (Wide World)

episode was wisely kept from the peacefully sleeping pilots. They were to be told about it only after the race the following day—a race, incidentally, which would be watched by over *one million* spectators!

The Solent was crammed with thousands upon thousands of boats of every conceivable type, from dinghys to ocean liners which had stopped to offer their passengers grandstand seats. Somehow a mile-wide corridor was maintained for the aircraft to fly over. It seemed that at least half the population of Britain had gathered along every bit of land adjacent to the course that wasn't vertical.

At about ten-thirty those near the base at Calshot saw, or at least heard, Waghorn's S-6 getting her final run up as she was being lowered onto the transport pontoon for the two-mile trip to the start. At two the starting gun aboard the *Medea* was fired and the 1929 race for the Schneider Trophy was on.

Waghorn's flatter propeller lifted him easily off the water, and two minutes later he swept into his first lap, carefully watching his temperature gauge. Even while holding his revs down Waghorn cut his first, and slowest lap, at 324 m.p.h.— and once again a Schneider racer's average around a course exceeded the outright world speed record. Waghorn had the

Waghorn's S-6 being run up on the day before the race.

Monti's M-67 on the slipway at Calshot. (Flight International)

race to himself for four laps before Dal Molin's Macchi M-52 joined him, its Fiat engine producing an ear-splitting scream which contrasted strongly with the thundering boom of "Wagger's" Rolls. By the time Waghorn had completed the course, at 328.63 m.p.h., the race was virtually decided. Cadringher's terrifying M-67 couldn't even catch Dal Molin's old M-52. Running very roughly and trailing a cloud of oily smoke, Cadringher retired on his first lap all but blinded and choked by his exhaust. Atcherley, who was going faster than anybody else, cut a pylon on his first lap (his goggles blew away) which later resulted in his disqualification, though he did set a 100-kilometer record at 332 m.p.h. on his last laps. Greig in the S-5 was having a great race with Dal Molin's M-52, these two 1927 aircraft being very closely matched, though the Italian seemed to be a shade faster.

The Italians' last hope was Monti. As his M-67 was ending its first lap at 301 m.p.h., instead of turning he flew serenely on and then landed! Poor Monti. No one knew then that a radiator pipe had burst and he had been severely scalded about his legs and hands. In terrible pain, he was helped from his aircraft and taken to the base hospital. Dal Molin was the only challenger to finish the course. He took second place at 284.11 m.p.h., Greig was third at 282.00 m.p.h.

On the following Tuesday, September 10, Stainforth and Orlebar, both having had enough of spectating, calmly went

Waghorn's S-6 N-247 in full song. (Flight International)

A mechanic runs up the eighteen-cylinder, broad-arrow type Isotta-Fraschini engine of Cadringher's Macchi M-67. (Flight International)

out and set up more world speed records. Stainforth was first at 330.3 m.p.h. in a Gloster-Napier, followed by Orlebar in Waghorn's S-6 N-247 thirty minutes later at 355.8 m.p.h. Curiously, neither of them seemed satisfied with this, and two days later Orlebar bumped it up again to 357.7 m.p.h.—in 1929!

Within a few months the pilots comprising this High-Speed Flight were all posted away to less stimulating assignments, only Orlebar and Stainforth remaining at Felixstowe. Just as everyone was beginning to relax at last, the Air Ministry shattered the peace with an announcement. Due to "sufficient data having now been collected for practical development in this area" they would no longer provide financial support for the construction of Schneider entries, nor would they allow R.A.F. personnel to fly them. It was going to be a long, hard pull to September 1931, and before then five Schneider pilots would be dead.

The Thompson Trophy— 1930

Late in 1929 it was announced that Charles E. Thompson, president of Cleveland's Thompson Products, Inc., had received the official sanction of the National Aeronautic Association to establish a trophy which would encourage the development of faster land-based aircraft. The mountains of money spent by various governments over the past seven or eight years in an effort to win the Schneider Trophy had resulted in the world's fastest aircraft being seaplanes—a situation demonstrating impressive technical achievement, but of limited practical value.

The new Thompson Trophy races were to be completely open, anything-goes events, with no limitation on fuels, superchargers, number or types of engines, and they would be open to both civil and military aircraft. The air ministries of England, France, Germany, Italy, Japan, and Spain had also been invited to enter. In addition, considerable prize money was to be offered, and though no one expected to recoup all expenses of entering, it was certainly a lot better than nothing.

From now on, in each succeeding year up to 1939, the races for the Thompson Trophy were to be the feature events at the close of the National Air Races. They were also to be the making of the air-cooled radial engine.

By the afternoon of September 1, the last day of the ten-day 1930 National Air Races, all the aircraft which were to fly in the first Thompson had arrived at Curtiss-Reynolds Airport at Chicago. All but one, that is; a stubby little biplane from the E. M. Laird Airplane Company. The reason that it

Waghorn rounding one of the mark-boats. (UPI)

wasn't there was a simple one. It hadn't been put together yet.

A frantic three weeks before the opening of the races in Chicago, Lee Schoenhair, chief of the aviation division of the B. F. Goodrich Rubber Company, placed an order with the Laird firm for an aircraft that he could fly in the Thompson. Matty Laird, the leading light of the organization and a man with a remarkable gift for laying out fast, stable aircraft, assured Schoenhair that his entry would be ready in time, but nobody really believed him.

At three-thirty on the afternoon of the race the last nut was tightened and the Laird "Solution" was rolled out into the sunlight of Ashburn Field, Chicago—home of the Laird company. (The crew had worked the last thirty-five hours without a break.) Wasting no time, Charles "Speed" Holman, a man who had stunted a Ford Trimotor the previous year, worked himself into the seat, started up the 300 h.p. Pratt-Whitney Wasp Junior, and calmly watched the needles wiggle on the dials in front of him as the aircraft came to life.

After a very brief warmup, Holman rolled the ship out onto the field, did a short, fast taxi run over the grass, shoved home the throttle, and roared into the air.

The flight lasted only a few minutes. Holman touched down again and taxied over to the nervous, exhausted group by the hangar and switched off. The expectant, red-eyed, unshaven faces waited for the word . . . Holman nodded. "It's fast," he said.

Five minutes later he was flying the "Solution" across town to Curtiss Reynolds Airport. (Schoenhair had been argued out of flying the aircraft himself by friends who wished to have him around a little longer. Holman knew all the habits of Laird aircraft, and had already flown several earlier races on the course which would be used for the Thompson.)

Ben Howard, a U.S. Air Mail pilot, had built an extremely clean, Gipsy-powered aircraft he had fondly christened "Pete." It had been constructed during eight months' spare time. Howard had set out to see just how much performance he could get from 90 h.p., and the result must have startled even the designer. "Pete" turned out to have an uncannily forgiving temperament and a top speed of over 200 m.p.h.!

Everything on "Pete" had been built to an irreducible minimum, though Howard's claim that he couldn't get into it if he was wearing heavy socks or underwear can probably be discounted. "Pete" had already won five of the lesser closed-course events and had collected nearly four thousand dollars in the bargain. The idea of entering this 90 h.p. gnat in the Thompson Trophy race had caused a lot of laughter to begin with. The smiles were now fading fast.

This year the U.S. Marine Corps was going to make a bid to restore some of the Air Services' dignity that was so thoroughly punctured by Doug Davis' Travel Air in 1929. Their

Benny Howard with his amazing little "Pete." Jimmy Haizlip's Travel Air can be seen in the background. (UPI)

entry was a much-revised, five-year-old U. S. Navy Curtiss Hawk. This same aircraft had won the Curtiss Marine Trophy in 1928, and again in May of the current year. Captain Arthur Page had flown it to this last win, and was to fly it also in this year's Thompson.

The Hawk's lower wing had been removed altogether, and a colossal 800 h.p. Curtiss "Conqueror" had replaced its normal D-12. The upper wing had been stiffened and was now fitted with the marvelous Curtiss wing radiators. Now designated type XF6C-6, this aircraft looked very difficult to beat.

Also entered were two "sport" examples of the brilliant Travel Air "R" which had caused all that fuss the year before. They were to be flown by Jimmy Haizlip, who had also won a couple of races in the last few days, and by Frank Hawks, who had recently set a new transcontinental record of 12 hours, 25 minutes, 3 seconds in his.

Rounding off the seven entries was Erett Williams in a Wedell-Williams (the racing world was soon to hear much more about *these* aircraft), and Paul Adams in a Travel Air "Speedwing" biplane.

Holman's Laird "Solution" arrived at the line barely in time. The aircraft were immediately put under starter's orders and, after the pilots had signaled they were ready, were given the starting signal at ten-second intervals.

Page's thundering Curtiss was first away, followed by Hawks' Travel Air, Howard's "Pete," Haizlip's Travel Air, Williams' Wedell-Williams, Holman's "Solution," and Adams' "Speedwing."

It was immediately clear that Page was going to run away with the race. He was already starting his second lap as Adams was taking off, and he gradually began to pull away from the field, averaging around 205 m.p.h. per lap.

Hawks had to retire with fuel feed problems on his fourth lap, and Williams was forced down with engine bothers on his eighth round. The story of the first Thompson Trophy race might well have ended this way, with Page putting the civilians back in their place and winning the race in a canter. But it was not to be.

As Page was rounding the home pylon in front of the stands on his seventeenth lap, his aircraft was seen to waver, go into a slow roll, and smash into the field, raising a fifty-foot cloud of dirt. Page was rushed to the airport hospital, and then to Evanston General Hospital, where he died of brain injuries. As yet no satisfactory cause has ever been offered to explain this tragedy, though it has been suggested that he may have succumbed to carbon monoxide poisoning.

Holman and Haizlip came home in that order, followed by Howard's amazing little "Pete." Their averages were 201.9, 199.8, and 162.8 m.p.h. respectively. Paul Adams also finished, averaging 142.6.

In a little over six months, Holman himself was killed in a minor race at Omaha. Though it was generally accepted that air racing was the best possible medicine for an ailing aviation industry, no one could dispute the fact that the cost sometimes seemed terribly high.

Captain Arthur Page's very clean, but dangerous, Curtiss XF6C-6. (UPI)

Charles "Speed" Holman, winner of the first race for the Thompson Trophy. (Wide World)

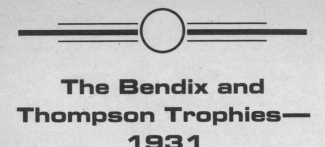

The Bendix and
Thompson Trophies—
1931

Ever since Calbraith P. Rodgers made the first transcontinental flight in a Wright biplane in 1911, American pilots had been relentlessly cutting down the time required to get from one end of the U.S.A. to the other. Rodgers' trip took forty-nine days and was attended by every imaginable type of misfortune—from flying into trees and fences to exploding engines. Only a few traces of his original aircraft were left by the time he reached California.

By 1923 Lieutenant John Macready had reduced the time to 26 hours, 50 minutes, and by 1930 Frank Hawks' Travel Air "R" had lowered it to 12 hours, 25 minutes. Though public interest in these fast flights across the country had always been considerable, it was about to get a tremendous boost. In 1931 Vincent Bendix, president of the Bendix Aviation Corporation, offered a new trophy for an annual, free-for-all transcontinental speed dash that was to rival the Thompson in importance.

The Bendix Trophy was to be run during the National Air Races, from the West Coast to Cleveland, now the permanent home of these events, and prize money totaling fifteen thousand dollars would also be paid to the first three finishers this year.

At a little after 2 A.M. on the morning of September 4, the floodlights at United Airport, Burbank, California, cast a hard, white light on the eight entries in this first race for the Bendix Trophy. Bad weather had already forced several postponements, but it looked as though this time they were going to get away.

If sheer numbers had anything to do with it, the odds were

that the winning aircraft would be from Lockheed—all but two entries had been built by this company. There were two "Orion" low-wing monoplanes to be flown by Harold Johnson and Beeler Blevins, three "Altair" types (a high-performance version of the "Orion") to be flown by Lou Reichers, James Hall, and Captain Ira Eaker, and the high-wing "Vega" belonging to Art Goebel, winner of the 1927 Dole Race. All these aircraft were powered by Pratt & Whitney "Wasp" variants, with Walter Hunter's Travel Air "R" (Doug Davis' 1929 winner) wearing a "Wasp Junior."

The remaining entrant was Jimmy Doolittle with his Laird "Super Solution," a brand-new, refined version of Holman's 1930 Thompson-winning biplane, powered by a "Wasp Junior" now developing some 510 h.p. This was a much prettier aircraft than its predecessor, with cleaner lines, an enclosed undercarriage with spats over the wheels, and a neat, green paint job with yellow trim. It was also very fast.

At 2:30 A.M. the pilots were all abroad, with engines fitfully booming, ready to go. At two-thirty-five the first starting signal was given and the maiden voyage for the Bendix Trophy was under way.

The aircraft were sent away at intervals just long enough to ensure that they wouldn't tangle with each other at the dark end of the runway, and within a few minutes their only trace was a faint drone from the inky sky as they thundered eastward.

To no one's surprise, Jimmy Doolittle soon took charge of the situation. Blevins, who had taken off just before Doolittle, said afterward that he saw Doolittle's Laird shoot past him so fast that he caught himself instinctively checking his air speed to see if he was on the verge of stalling!

As had happened so often before, and would happen again, it was Jimmy Doolittle all the way. After touching down briefly for fuel at Albuquerque and Kansas City, he landed at Cleveland, in a mild drizzle, where the National Air Races had been under way for five days. His time for the trip was 9 hours, 10 minutes, 21 seconds.

Next in was Harold Johnson's "Orion" in 10 hours, 14 minutes, 22 seconds, followed by Blevins' "Orion" in 10:49:33. Eaker was fourth in 10:59:43, followed by Goebel and Hall in 11:53:48 and 12:51:16, respectively.

Lou Reichers' "Altair" ran out of fuel over Beatrice, Nebraska, and Walter Hunter's Travel Air suffered a small fire at Terre Haute, Indiana. He was to have more fire troubles soon.

Some people might have been satisfied to stop in Cleveland, but not Jimmy Doolittle. He was in a fine position to break Hawks' transcontinental record, and to collect the extra twenty-five hundred dollars offered by Bendix for doing it. After assisting in the refueling operation, and politely declining the sandwich and bottle of milk hopefully proferred by his wife who had been waiting for his arrival, he settled back into the cockpit, roared over the muddy field, lifted off, and disappeared into a thunderhead.

Eleven hours, 16 minutes, and 10 seconds after he had left Burbank, Doolittle touched down at Newark Airport, chopping over an hour off Frank Hawks' transcontinental record, winning the first Bendix Trophy, seventy-five hundred dollars, and the twenty-five hundred dollars to boot.

Then he flew all the way back to Cleveland. Later that afternoon he flew out of Cleveland to St. Louis. Then he flew back to Cleveland the following day.

One might have wondered if he was ever going to stay on the ground long enough to spend any of the money.

The National Air Races had been in progress since August 29, before daily crowds of around thirty-seven thousand. It had been decided this year to hold qualifying trials for the Thompson. These consisted of four runs over a mile-long straightaway in front of the grandstands. A lower limit of 175 m.p.h. was imposed to keep the number of entries down by eliminating all but the faster aircraft.

By the eve of the race eight entrants had qualified. Doolittle had put his "Super Solution" through the traps at 255.345 m.p.h., and his fastest run was over 272 m.p.h. This might have been enough to sow seeds of despair in the hearts of all the other entries, were it not for a shattering surprise that had occurred back on September 1.

Lowell Bayles, a commercial pilot from Springfield, Massachusetts, had qualified the first example of one of the most famous, and infamous, racing aircraft of all time—the amazing Gee Bee Model Z.

Built by Granville Brothers Aircraft, also of Springfield, the

Doolittle refueling his Laird ''Solution'' at Cleveland. (UPI)

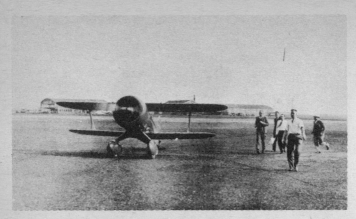

Doolittle touches down at Newark Airport after chopping over an hour off Hawks' transcontinental record. (UPI)

Model Z had been designed and built with but one objective: to win the 1931 Thompson. The money to finance its construction had been charmed and cajoled from investors all over Springfield and beyond, and the Springfield Air Racing Association had been formed to keep things on a business-like basis. Backers would share in the winnings, if any, according to their investment.

Model Z was designed by Bob Hall, with assorted ideas thrown in by Bayles (who had also contributed five hundred dollars to the cause) and the five Granville brothers. With the work being carried out in the shop often only minutes behind the designing being done in the office, and the bills often ahead of both, Model Z was completed on the afternoon of August 2.

It looked like no aircraft ever seen before. It was only 15 feet long, shorter than a decent-size automobile, with a wingspan of 23½ feet, a good third of which was swallowed up in the fuselage. It really didn't look as though it could fly, despite the fact that the nose was stuffed with a 535 h.p. supercharged "Wasp Junior."

But fly it did, and in no uncertain fashion. Bayles qualified this aircraft for the Thompson at 267.242 m.p.h., with one run at over 286, and it wasn't running well at the time either. This was not only nearly 12 m.p.h. faster than Doolittle's qualifying speed, it was the first time since 1924 that Bonnet's landplane record of 278.48 m.p.h. seemed within striking distance.

Walter Hunter's Travel Air was going again after his fire problems during the Bendix flight. He also attempted to qualify along with Doolittle on September 6. During his first run, at well over 200 m.p.h. and at 200 feet, his aircraft was suddenly covered in flames due to a fuel leak. He jumped, and his chute opened only a few feet before he hit the ground. He was rushed immediately to the field hospital, painfully but not seriously burned. It was barely two months before he was up and flying again.

By the time the Thompson was about to be run, on the afternoon of September 7, aircraft built by the young Granville organization had won five of the major races out of a total of thirty-four, and in all the races but one that they had entered and *not* won, they had placed second or third.

Granville designer Bob Hall takes the Model Z up for its first flight. (Wide World)

The other six qualifiers were now receiving their final touches. Another Gee Bee, a Model Y, was to be flown by Bob Hall, the Granville designer. Jimmy Wedell was to fly the first example of a new Wedell-Williams design—a sleek, low-wing layout which would prove extremely effective in the years to come.

Lee Schoenhair seemed fated never to fly in the Thompson. Talked out of it the previous year (with good reason), he now had been put to bed with nervous exhaustion, having burned a little too much midnight oil in an effort to get his Laird "Solution" ready again. His friend Dale Jackson was to fly it for him.

Bill Ong was to fly a Laird "Speedwing," and Captain Eaker was to pilot his Lockheed "Altair," which had taken fourth spot in the Bendix. Ben Howard, back again with "Pete," had just barely managed to qualify, in the middle of a downpour, at 176.24 m.p.h., or about 100 m.p.h. too slow to be in contention. Nonetheless, "Pete" was still the darling of the crowd, and had already won twenty-five hundred dollars from his bigger brothers anyway.

Immediately after the preceding race had ended (in the course of which "Pete" bagged another $720), the aircraft which were to fly in the Thompson were run out to the starting line directly in front of the grandstands. With engines ticking over, the mechanics, owners, and pilots fidgeted as the last few minutes dragged them toward the moment they had spent all their time, and in some cases all their money, preparing for.

At last the stand-by signal was given, the thunder of seven engines swept across the field, and suddenly Ben Howard's "Pete" tore away from the line, followed at ten-second intervals by Bayles, Wedell, Eaker, Jackson, Doolittle, and Ong.

By the time they were returning from the scattering pylon Bayles' Gee Bee was already leading, and Doolittle was storming up from behind, already halfway through the field. At the end of the first lap Bayles was still in the lead with an average of 207 m.p.h. Wedell's aircraft was showing a surprising turn of speed—216 m.p.h. on his first lap and also closing up on Bayles. Doolittle was just behind.

Bayles was only getting the feel of his mount though. He opened the tap a bit more on his second tour and his lap speed jumped to 222.77 m.p.h. By now Doolittle was just behind him, and Wedell was also beginning to catch up again with a lap of 224.33 m.p.h. Bayles was flying a very cool race, only using as much of his aircraft as was necessary, and he had plenty in hand. He shoved the throttle forward another couple of notches.

The Gee Bee responded immediately by jumping its lap speeds up around the 240 m.p.h. mark and drawing away from the pack. Meanwhile Dale Jackson had flown Schoenhair's "Solution" through the top of an oak tree on his fifth lap. Luckily, he managed to keep it in the air even though the structure and fabric of the lower wing was in shreds and its neat white paint job was now trimmed with green.

Doolittle's engine, the same "Wasp Junior" that had run flat-out faultlessly for over three thousand miles, decided to give up on the sixth lap. It first began to overheat, then a thin trail of smoke appeared and power began to drop fast. There was no alternative, so Doolittle pulled off the course on his seventh lap and landed, losing a race for once.

Bayles went on to win the 1931 Thompson Trophy, and the seventy-five-hundred-dollar kitty, with an average of 236.239 m.p.h. Jimmy Wedell was second with an average of 228 m.p.h., a speed which netted him forty-five hundred dollars. Jackson brought Schoenhair's oak leaf-decorated "Solution" in for a remarkable third place, and winning three thousand dollars, some of which would pay for the damage.

After Jackson came Bob Hall in the model "Y" at 201.251, Ira Eaker's "Altair" at 196.821, Ben Howard's "Pete" at 163.573, and Bill Ong at 153.049 m.p.h. Eaker flew around for a while after the race trying to shake his undercarriage down. It wouldn't budge though, and he finally had to come down without it. It was very well handled, and the damage was only superficial.

The winning speed this year was about 35 m.p.h. faster than in 1930—quite a jump, but it was to go a lot higher.

Early in the morning on the day of the Thompson, Bayles had attempted to set a new record for landplanes, but nothing seemed to work right. The Gee Bee's engine began to lose power and the timing apparatus packed in, so the next try was put forward to the following day. This attempt was also aban-

The violent end of Lowell Bayles and the Model Z. Bayles' body can be seen between the wreckage and the car at left. (UPI)

doned when two Granville mechanics were injured in a high-way accident near Ashtabula, Ohio. Bayles dropped everything to fly them back to the hospital in Springfield.

The record attempt was held up through one thing or another until the following December 5. At about 1 P.M. Bayles took off from Wayne Airport outside Detroit to make his third try of the afternoon (a faulty barograph and engine problems had washed out the others).

The Model Z had by now been fitted with an immense 800 h.p. "Wasp" and had been carefully, though unofficially, timed at just over 314 m.p.h.

Bayles wound the Gee Bee up to full speed and flashed through the starting trap about 150 feet above the ground. He was about halfway through when it happened . . .

The fuel-filler cap in front of the cockpit was torn off by the blast of the airstream, smashing the windshield into Bayles' face. Blinded, he tried for altitude but the sudden load snapped the spar in the right wing. The aircraft whirled around in two lightning rolls and smashed into a railway embankment. The huge engine wrenched itself free and tore off alongside the track for several hundred feet. Nothing but scattered shreds of the aircraft were left.

Bayles was thirty-one years old.

The Schneider Trophy— 1931

At long last, at an F.A.I. meeting in Paris on January 17, 1930, it was moved and adopted that the tiresome watertightness and navigability tests be permanently dropped from the Schneider contests. They had long outlived their purpose, which was simply to promote the development of seaworthy aircraft, and everyone concerned was glad to see the end of them. It was agreed that they would be replaced by a "simple" takeoff and alighting test under full load with a run on the surface lasting not less than two minutes. This would be more than sufficient to prove the aircraft seaworthy.

As this welcome news was filtering through to the various teams on the following afternoon, sudden tragedy again struck the Italian team. Dal Molin, while flying the twin-tandem-engined Savoia-Marchetti S-65 at high speed and low altitude over Lake Garda, was killed instantly as his aircraft suddenly plunged into the water, without any apparent reason. This accident was strongly reminiscent of the manner in which Kinkead had died, and no definite cause has ever been attributed to either incident.

As yet the British weren't sure whether they would be contesting another Schneider or not. The Air Ministry was resolutely sticking by its guns on the issue of no more public funds for the Schneider contests, although it had stated that it would allow a qualified individual or group to "borrow" the existing aircraft for the 1931 contest. As no one had come forward by well into February of that year, many Englishmen were contemplating the humiliating situation of having a foreign challenger come to England, fly around the course unopposed, and take home the Trophy. In fact, the Royal Aero Club had suggested at an F.A.I. meeting that the contest should be postponed for a time. Italy and France, among others, quite rightly objected to this as they had already been preparing for some time. The future looked pretty black for the British.

Then, as from a fairytale storybook, the remarkable person of Lady Houston, D.B.E., entered upon the scene. Highly indignant that the British were unable to contest the Trophy, and determined "to prevent the Socialist Government from being spoil-sports," she announced that she would put up one hundred thousand pounds to see that the thing was done properly. In today's money this comes to something over three-quarters of a million dollars!

Things immediately began to happen after Lady Houston's remarkable gift was gratefully accepted by the Royal Aero Club. After the issue went all the way up to the Prime Minister (Ramsay MacDonald), it was decided that the R.A.F. would be permitted once more to handle the defense of the Trophy.

It was almost like old times again.

The High-Speed Flight was reformed at once, again under the skilled command of Orlebar, and another training program was under way. The new team consisted of Flight Lieutenants E. J. L. Hope, F. W. Long, J. N. Boothman, and G. H. Stainforth (the one remaining member of the 1929 Flight), Flying Officers L. S. Smith and R. L. Brinton, who was on loan from the Royal Navy. Flight Lieutenant W. F. Dry was Engineering Officer.

Just as the training program was getting under way, the entire nation was shocked by the news that Waghorn, the winner of the 1929 contest, had been killed while testing a Hawker Horsley for the Experimental Section at Farnborough on May 5. In sudden trouble at low altitude, he had waited for his passenger to bail out, after which he attempted to do so himself. His chute didn't have time to open, but his passenger was saved.

Boothman had a near thing himself just before Christmas. He had taken up Kinkead's old Gloster 4-B for a spin and stalled it over the water. The aircraft plowed into the surface and sank immediately. Very luckily for Boothman the fuselage was broken open just where he was sitting and he was able to

The British team form up in front of one of the new S-6B's. Left to right: E. J. L. Hope, R. L. Brinton, F. W. Long, G. H. Stainforth, A. H. Orlebar, J. N. Boothman, L. S. Smith and W. F. Dry. (National Archives)

get out. Boothman's flying in the Gloster 4-A had been flawless, and it was felt that a momentary lack of orientation in the rather thin fog had caused his accident.

Two brand-new and revised Supermarine S-6's were to be built for the forthcoming Schneider event and the 1929 aircraft would be brought up to their specification, but it was the French who were giving cause for a good bit of concern in both the British and Italian camps. Their very advanced 1929 airframes had received meticulous revision, and a superb range of new engines had been produced. The Lorraine organization had come up with a magnificent supercharged inverted V-12 of 2200 h.p. called the "Radium" engine. Renault had conjured a blown V-12 of some 2300 h.p., and Hispano-Suiza had now brought their model 18-Sb up to over 1900 horses. Eventually the Lorraine and Hisso designs were chosen, and were handed over to Nieuport-Delage and Bernard, respectively. Also, a gleaming all-metal Dewoitine with Lorraine power was being prepared. These aircraft were aiming at speeds up to four hundred miles per hour, and if France ever looked like winning another Schneider, it was now—if only they could get them ready in time.

The French pilots had also been announced. After some confusion, their team stood as follows: Commander Amaurich of the French Navy was in charge, with Captains Marly and Vernold, Lieutenants Bougault and Roturna, and Sergeants Baillet, Goussin, and Labreveux, as pilots. While awaiting the actual racing aircraft, they were training on 1000 h.p. Bernard H.V.-42's, which was one tough aircraft to train on. A group of highly experienced civilian pilots, headed by Sadi Lecointe, would first wring out the racing machines before handing them over to the French team. Their training was again based at Berre, near Marseilles.

Some time earlier, actually back in September 1930, the Americans announced that they would not enter this year. Much more financing would now be necessary than any private individual or group was prepared to meet—people like Lady Houston don't happen very often—and even if they found the money they stood only a slim chance of winning now. One of the things money can't buy is experience.

The French Hispano-Suiza-powered Bernard which was not completed in time. (National Archives)

A Renault-engined Nieuport Delage at the French training camp at Berre, near Marseilles. (National Archives)

On March 23 the Royal Aero Club announced that the 1931 Schneider Trophy contest would be held on Saturday, September 12, again over the Solent. Now once again, everybody had a date to aim for.

On July 3 Freddie Hope took the newly arrived S-6A out for their first spin together. Once in flight an engine cowling suddenly came loose and threatened to tear itself free and smash the tail. As soon as he noticed it Hope switched off and tried to put down near a Dutch passenger liner. The moment he touched down his aircraft was tossed skyward again by the liner's swell. He tried to catch it again with a burst of engine, but the aircraft fell back again and cartwheeled into the sea. Amazingly, Hope was only slightly injured, but it took divers two days to find the aircraft.

By mid-July the first new S-6B had been delivered to Calshot. There was a minor panic shortly afterward when Orlebar discovered, after repeated attempts, that it just wouldn't lift off the water! The difficulty was eventually traced to the new short-diameter propeller. When an effort was made to get the old 9'6″ type again they were told that there simply weren't any, and that the molds in which they had been cast had been broken up! There were a lot of grim faces around Calshot until they were told that the new blanks could be forged out to the old length.

Although there wasn't a great deal of dependable information concerning the Italian and French teams, it was believed that both their training programs were on schedule, and that both teams would appear in full force for the contest. Tragically, within three consecutive days both teams received crippling blows. On July 31, Lieutenant Bougault of the French High-Speed Flight was testing one of the magnificent Bernard racers at low level over l'Étang-de-Berre. Suddenly a propeller blade let go, and after a few terrible moments it was all over. Then on August 2, the redoubtable Giovanni Monti, who had made so many friends in England in 1929, hit the surface of Lake Garda at nearly 400 m.p.h. It took four weeks to find his body.

On August 18, Jerry Brinton of the Royal Navy had his first flight in S-6A N-247. As his aircraft lifted clear, Brinton instinctively eased the stick forward. It was his last mistake. The aircraft fell back onto the surface, bounced, fell again, leaped to about thirty feet, and then plunged to the bottom. The force of the impact slammed Brinton all the way back under the vertical fin oil tank in the tail. He was still strapped to the seat when they found him.

On September 4, only a week before race day, the French and Italian teams formally withdrew from the contest. The loss of aircraft and personnel had seriously undermined their strength, and they needed time to reorganize. They tried to get the Royal Aero Club to agree to a postponement, without success. The British team *was* ready, and it was remembered that both the French and Italians had refused a postponement at Britain's request only a few months before. Britain would now fly what would be the final Schneider race—unopposed. Since this would also be her third successive victory, the Schneider races were all but ended.

On race day, a Saturday, the weather was so bad that a postponement had to be called anyway, and the event was put forward to the next day. There was now no reason for more than one aircraft to fly the course, so the pilots were ranked according to their length of service with the Flight. As there was also to be a record attempt following the fly-over, Stainforth got his choice of either one. He chose the record, so Boothman got to fly the last of the Schneider courses. Naturally, everybody wanted to have a bash, but there was no sense in subjecting men and machines to unnecessary risk.

At two minutes past one o'clock on the afternoon of the following Sunday John Boothman's S-6B S-1595 was launched from its barge, and the last Schneider race was under way. Boothman flew the course without an error, averaging 340.08 m.p.h. for the distance.

At four that afternoon Stainforth took S-1596 out for the record. He made five runs over the three kilometers, and his best four averaged 379.05 m.p.h., again not quite the kind of speed he had hoped for. Stainforth wasn't too disappointed, though, as he planned to make another attempt within the next few days as soon as a special sprint engine was ready. On the following Wednesday, September 16, Stainforth was testing a new propeller on S-1596 when his left heel jammed in the rudder controls as he was touching down. The aircraft responded instantly by cartwheeling and then plunging in upside down. Luckily Stainforth managed to free his foot and get to the surface.

On September 29, after a false start a few days before, he took Boothman's S-1595 up for another shot at the record. The special sprint engine that had been prepared for the record attempt had demonstrated a distressing tendency to explode under full power, so it had been dropped for this attempt and the aircraft was more or less in its standard form. Its engine had been reconditioned, and the only departures from standard specifications were the fitting of a rather exotic propeller and the use of a foul-smelling, methanol-based fuel.

The combination seemed to be the right one. Flight Lieutenant George Stainforth became the first man in history to officially exceed 400 m.p.h. The first four of his five runs over the three-kilometer course averaged 407.5 m.p.h., and he had covered his first trip at over 415 m.p.h. It was the perfect note on which to end the great Schneider series.

Though the contests were now ended, the Italians continued to develop their 1931 machines, one of which was the now famous Macchi-Castoldi MC-72. This fantastic aircraft with twin Fiat AS-6 engines back-to-back driving concentric contra-

Rain, choppy seas and poor visibility combined to force the cancellation of the race as originally scheduled for Saturday, September 12th. It was put forward to the next day. (Flight International)

Mechanics working over Agello's formidable Macchi-Castoldi MC-72 shortly before its record-shattering run of 440.67 m.p.h. The record stands to this day. (UPI)

rotating propellers boosted the new world record to 423 m.p.h. on April 10, 1933. It was flown by Francesco Agello, a warrant officer now and the only remaining pilot of the 1929 team. Just to drive home the point, on the following June 2, Agello got an official, and quite incredible, 440.67 m.p.h. in this aircraft. This record for propeller-driven seaplanes stands to this day, and probably always will.

The Bendix and Thompson Trophies— 1932

This year the three most successful builders of racing aircraft in America were to make determined efforts to take both the Bendix and Thompson races.

Doolittle revised his fierce little biplane, which by now might well have been called the Super-Super Solution, but wasn't. Its P&W Wasp Junior was replaced by a Wasp of undisclosed power, but it certainly must have been well over 700 h.p. The one other major alteration was the installation of a new re-tractable landing gear. These two revisions alone probably added about 65 m.p.h. to it, and its target of 300 m.p.h. seemed almost a foregone conclusion.

But there were others who were aiming at the 300 m.p.h. mark. The Granville organization had begun the construction of two new aircraft, outwardly similar, but intended for two widely differing purposes; the Thompson and the Bendix. Both were based on Bayles' Model Z, but both were even more startling. One was powered by a new P&W Wasp developing some 800 h.p. and carried just enough fuel to take it about 200 miles in a hurry. The other was fitted with a Wasp Junior of about 535 h.p. It had a range of about 450–500 miles. They were to be flown by Russell Boardman and Lee Ghelbach, though Boardman actually owned both aircraft.

These two machines, designated R-1 and R-2, were the logical (if that is the word) extension of the ideas that had resulted in the Model Z, but carried out with a great deal more attention to detail, and to theory. For instance, wind-tunnel tests had shown that for maximum penetration (at 300 m.p.h.)

the diameter of the tubby fuselage should be considerably greater than the engine cowling, and that this point should occur about one-third of the way back from the nose. This was in complete opposition to current practice, but in the thirties many aerodynamic "laws" were subject to change without notice. In this case the theory was borne out in practice: the penetration was excellent—but the directional control was terrible.

This year Jimmy Wedell was taking a more conventional route, simply revising in detail his Wedell-Williams "44" of 1931. Back in the spring of 1931 Wedell and Roscoe Turner had worked together on the design of a low-wing racer, suitable for cross-country or closed-course events, and capable of handling a large increase in power without too much revision. One example was built for Turner, powered by a 535 h.p. Wasp Junior, and although Turner didn't race it that year Wedell was so impressed with it that he promptly built one for himself—and had chased Bayles home with it in the 1931 Thompson.

Lee Ghelbach and the R-2 shortly after their arrival at Cleveland. (UPI)

The biggest advantage this design turned out to have, apart from its speed, was its handling; it was flawless. This was a rare enough quality for *any* aircraft in 1931—in a racer it was (except for "Pete") unheard of. Jimmy Haizlip had also been impressed by "44," and one more was built for him. Now there were three of them, and all were entered in the forthcoming Bendix race.

There was one additional entry in this year's Bendix. Claire Vance, a highly experienced air-mail pilot, was to enter a semi-flying-wing transport aircraft that had a range of over five thousand miles, in theory, anyway. With a maximum of about 210 m.p.h. it could obviously make the trip from Burbank to Cleveland non-stop, and might well make up for its speed deficiency in this way.

Once again the start of the Bendix was delayed several times. The first holdup was due to the non-arrival of some of the entries; then the weather delayed them for a while.

At the start in the early morning of August 29 were Turner, Haizlip, and Wedell in their virtually identical aircraft, Lee Ghelbach's Gee Bee R-2, and Claire Vance's flying wing (Doolittle wasn't able to make it, but more of that shortly). As the aircraft were sent away from Burbank one by one, each with his own independent route to Cleveland, it didn't seem too likely that Doolittle's record would fall this year, but Jimmy Haizlip, and the Shell Company, had other ideas.

All the entries but one had infuriating troubles en route. Vance's flying wing thing petered out early with a leaky fuel system and retired. Turner made two very quick stops at Colorado Springs and Quincy, Illinois on his way to Cleveland Airport, only to waste twenty minutes or so in Cleveland waiting for the idiot driver of the tank truck to drive over to him so he could fill up. Eventually Turner had to taxi over to the truck, with murder in his heart, and watch more time being wasted while a Chinese fire-drill routine was carried out during the fueling operation. He had been only a few minutes behind Haizlip when he arrived.

Wedell had a similar experience at Chicago Municipal Airport, only he lost forty minutes before he could find the right people to swear at.

Ghelbach's Gee Bee had touched down at Amarillo, Texas, and got away again quite quickly, but any advantage he might have gained over the others soon evaporated. On his way to Rantoul, Illinois he started losing oil and barely made it before running dry. An oil tank had split, and it took nearly an hour to fix it.

During all this grief and misery Haizlip's flight was rolling on, perfectly timed and beautifully organized. He had paused at Goodland, Kansas and Lansing, Illinois. On both stops, while his wheels were still turning, a Shell tanker was alongside and men were running the hose out to him. Neither stop took more than six minutes.

Haizlip didn't stop at Cleveland. He made a low pass over the field to get his time recorded and then set course for Floyd Bennett Field and a new transcontinental record. Haizlip touched down exactly 10 hours, 19 minutes after he had left Burbank, cutting almost an hour off Doolittle's record and averaging about 245 m.p.h. As he switched off and began climbing out, picking the cotton from his ears, he noticed that his was the only one of the Bendix entries there.

"Where is everybody . . . ?" he said.

Only Turner joined Haizlip at Floyd Bennett; the others stopped at Cleveland. Here are their times and prizes:

			Bendix	Transcont.	
1st	Jimmy Haizlip	Wedell-Williams	8:19:45	10:19	$6,750
2nd	Jimmy Wedell	Wedell-Williams	8:47:31		$3,750
3rd	Roscoe Turner	Wedell-Williams	9:02:25	10:58	$2,250
4th	Lee Ghelbach	Gee Bee R-2	9:41:39		$1,500

Early in 1932 it was announced that the qualifying speed for the Thompson (in what were now called the Shell Speed Dashes) had been raised to 200 m.p.h. It was clear that records were going to topple this year, and the field was formidable.

There were the Gee Bee's, R-1 and R-2, of Boardman and Ghelbach, and the three Wedell-Williams of Haizlip, Turner, and Wedell. Bob Hall had now left the Granville organization and had set up shop on his own at Agawam Field, also in Springfield. He had designed and built a gorgeous gull-wing Wasp-powered aircraft for Russell Thaw this year. It was his famous "Bulldog."

Ben Howard was back with "Pete," and two new giant-

Bob Hall's "Bulldog" that had been built for Russell Thaw. When it was completed Thaw tried a few flights in it and decided he didn't like it, so Hall flew it in the Thompson. (UPI)

Boardman with the R-1 shortly before his first flight. It can be seen that there was no vertical fin area at all above the rudder. Boardman found the Gee Bee violently unstable directionally during the first short hop, and the addition of fin area was the first modification to be carried out when the aircraft arrived back at Springfield. It didn't help much. (UPI)

killers, "Ike" and "Mike." These two new ones again followed Howard's principle of the irreducible minimum, and nobody was laughing this time.

Young Keith Rider, a San Francisco aeronautical engineer, was also applying science rather than brute force to get performance. His Menasco-powered "San Francisco I" had placed second to the Model Z Gee Bee in one of the lesser races at the Nationals in 1931. It was back again this year, a little cleaner, a little faster.

In mid-August, as last-minute preparations were under way, two incidents occurred that changed things drastically. Russell Boardman was injured when a Gee Bee "Sportster" spun in. He wasn't seriously hurt, but it was enough to keep him in the hospital for several weeks. The R-1 was now without a pilot, and though offers to fly it began coming in from all over, Boardman didn't like the sound of any of them. He had flown the R-1 just long enough and fast enough (275 m.p.h.) to realize that one mistake in this beast at high speed and low altitude would be the last one.

Doolittle meanwhile had been ironing the wrinkles out of his new Laird biplane. On August 23 he took it up over Wichita, Kansas to put a fine edge on the trim. After tossing it around for twenty minutes or so he started to crank down the new retractable undercarriage. It was jammed.

Doolittle spent the next two hours trying to shake, jerk, or jar it loose. He eventually managed to get one leg halfway down, but this was probably worse than nothing at all. When his tanks were nearly dry he brought it in on the grass at the edge of the airport. It was beautifully done of course, but the damage, though superficial, was extensive enough to keep it out of the Bendix and the Thompson. Boardman managed to get Doolittle on the phone on August 27, and Doolittle was in Springfield the following day.

As the world's greatest racing pilot slowly walked around the R-1, he kept firing off a steady stream of questions, and he knew them all. The Granville brothers supplied the answers, or most of them. After this had gone on for a while, Doolittle climbed inside and asked to be started up. One of the Granvilles asked gently where he was planning to go. Over the bark of the big Wasp came a voice from within this thing that no pilot

Doolittle inspects his Laird biplane after putting down at Wichita with a jammed undercarriage. (UPI)

Doolittle (standing in front of the wing, in shirt sleeves with back to camera) and the R-1 outside the Skyways hangar, shortly after their arrival at Cleveland. (UPI)

Doolittle brings the R-1 down after his successful attempt on the landplane record. (UPI)

in his right mind would have touched with a ten-foot pole . . . "I'm going to Cleveland of course!" And he did.

This year the National Air Races were flown from August 27 to September 5, with the Thompson held, as usual, on the closing day. The qualifying runs had been held over several days up to the eve of race day, and were the cause of a bit of excitement. This reached a peak on September 3 when Doolittle qualified the R-1 at 294.38 m.p.h., finally smashing Bonnet's long-standing record for landplanes, and collecting a handy $1575 for being the fastest qualifier.

Qualifying speeds—1932 Thompson:

Jimmy Doolittle	Gee Bee R-1	294.38 m.p.h.	$1,575
Jimmy Wedell	Wedell-Williams	277.057 m.p.h.	$875
Roscoe Turner	Wedell-Williams	266.674 m.p.h.	$525
Jimmy Haizlip	Wedell-Williams	266.440 m.p.h.	$350
Bob Hall	Hall "Bulldog"	243.717 m.p.h.	—
Ray Moore	Rider R-1	237.738 m.p.h.	—
Bill Ong	Howard "Ike"	213.855 m.p.h.	—
Les Bowen	Gordon Israel Spl.	202.490 m.p.h.	—

On the afternoon of September 5, just before the aircraft were to line up for the Thompson, Doolittle's R-1 gave a fine demonstration of its skittish temperament. As it was being started up it backfired, the fuel in the carburetor caught it, and in a few moments the entire front end of the aircraft was ablaze. It was rapidly put out, with Doolittle assisting. No apparent damage had resulted, except to the crew's nerves, so Doolittle got back into it, started up again, and rolled out to the line where eight of the world's fastest landplanes were waiting.

Once in position, the pilots were given the stand-by, and the roar became deafening as the grass quivered against the ground behind them. Hall was the first to break, followed at ten-second intervals by Doolittle, Moore, Wedell, Haizlip, Ghelbach, Turner, and Ong. Bowen was left on the line in a storm of dust with engine trouble.

Hall and Doolittle had controllable propellers that got them off the ground in half the distance the others took. Doolittle was already closing on Hall on the way back from the scattering pylon, and on the first lap he caught him. The only time the other entries saw Doolittle from then on was when he passed them, and he passed everybody but Jimmy Wedell at least once.

A ding-dong fight was taking place for third spot, however. Haizlip, Ghelbach, and Turner were in a clump some distance behind Wedell, and nobody was giving or getting an inch. Eventually, on the seventh lap, Turner managed to sneak around in front, just as Doolittle blasted past the pack of them. This was one the fans remembered.

1st	Jimmy Doolittle	Gee Bee R-1	252.686 m.p.h.	$4,500
2nd	Jimmy Wedell	Wedell-Williams	242.496 m.p.h.	$2,500
3rd	Roscoe Turner	Wedell-Williams	233.042 m.p.h.	$1,500
4th	Jimmy Haizlip	Wedell-Williams	231.304 m.p.h.	$1,000
5th	Lee Ghelbach	Gee Bee R-2	222.098 m.p.h.	$500
6th	Bob Hall	Hall "Bulldog"	215.570 m.p.h.	—
7th	Bill Ong	Howard "Ike"	191.073 m.p.h.	—

Ray Moore out on third lap—engine.

It is interesting to note that the first six aircraft finished in the order of their qualifying speeds. This could either mean

Jimmy Doolittle claims the Thompson Trophy, and the $4500 that came with it. (Acme)

that the pilot's skills were very evenly matched . . . or that skills didn't mean anything at all!

The crowd of about fifty-five thousand were cheering their heads off as Doolittle worked his way out of the R-1, having won the 1932 Thompson Trophy. As he was asking about the other pilots, Jimmy Haizlip's young son got through the tight little group and congratulated Doolittle on his win. "Thanks very much son," Doolittle said. "I only wish I'd flown as good a race as your dad did."

There, by God, was a man.

The Bendix and Thompson Trophies— 1933

After the Wedell-Williams' impressive performance in the 1932 Bendix, American air-racing *aficionados* now had something else to talk about besides the Gee Bee's. Later in 1932 these aircraft set several more fast cross-country times. Among them was Jimmy Wedell's flight from Ottawa to Washington, D.C. to Mexico City on October 23, in 11 hours, 53 minutes, breaking Doolittle's "three capitals" record of 12 hours, 36 minutes, set in his Super-Solution twelve months before.

Also, on November 14, Turner flew his "Gilmore 121" from New York to Burbank, taking the east-to-west transcontinental record (upwind all the way) from Frank Hawks with a time of 12 hours, 33 minutes.

By the spring of 1933 rumors were flying thick and fast as to what the Granvilles would come up with this year, and what Turner and Wedell would do about it. Some of the mystery was cleared up in late June when an aviation reporter managed to pry loose a little information. Turner's Wedell-Williams was now fitted with an 800 h.p. supercharged Wasp, and had undergone very thorough refinement. Wedell's "44" was apparently as before, still carrying its 535 h.p. Wasp Junior, but it was still an amazingly fast airplane (with equal power it was about 10–12 m.p.h. faster than the W-W's of Turner and Haizlip).

The Granvilles had taken a route similar to Turner's, but they had gone a little farther along it. Boardman's R-1 now carried a huge, 900 h.p. P&W Hornet, but was otherwise unaltered. The R-2 had now taken over R-1's Wasp and cowling, and had also acquired a new, larger wing with flaps, and a few detail changes. There still didn't seem to be anything in the air that could approach these four aircraft, and barring some sort of calamity, one of them was sure to be top dog in 1933.

This year the National Air Races were to be held in Los Angeles, the promoters having wrung most of the interest, and money, out of the Cleveland area. Also, the dreary processionals for light aircraft and closed, private types had at last been eliminated. Apart from being a dreadful bore they, along with the other silly events held over the past few years, had stretched the yearly race program to cover a full ten days— and each day the customers had to pay again to get in. It's no wonder the organizers were losing money. The race program had now been cut down to four days, and was to be held over July 1–4.

By the time all the entries had arrived at Floyd Bennett Field for the start of the Bendix on the evening of June 31, bad weather had also arrived. Though it wasn't raining too hard,

Boardman with the R-1 early in 1933. In an effort to get some sort of directional stability, the rudder area had been vastly increased. The aircraft by now had also been fitted with an even bigger P&W "Hornet." (UPI)

there was a very wet mist around, and it was anybody's guess when it would go away. Amelia Earhart Putnam, the famed transatlantic flyer, made the best of it by curling up on one of the waiting room couches while her husband argued with the weather people. Roscoe Turner spent the time avoiding a process server by disguising himself in overalls and a sailor hat and carrying a wrench wherever he went. At about 3 A.M. the process server and the fog withdrew, and the seven Bendix entries made ready to go.

Mrs. Putnam was to fly her famous red Lockheed Vega, hoping to cop the extra twenty-five hundred dollars in prize money offered this year in a special women's category. (Ruth Nichols, better known for her closed-course racing, was also to fly this year, but withdrew at the last moment.)

Russell Boardman and Russell Thaw were there, as were their revamped R-1 and R-2 Gee Bees. Both these aircraft could do an easy 300 m.p.h. now, and if they could keep going they would be very hard to beat. Also, there were the three Wedell-Williams racers of Turner, Wedell, and Lee Ghelbach (in Haizlip's "92"). Turner's aircraft was just beautiful now. No longer wearing its gaudy Gilmore paint, it was now resplendent in gold-bronze with red trim and carried racing number "2." Turner had already managed 317 m.p.h. with this little beauty, but he wasn't telling anybody just now.

Frank Hawks was acting as official starter this year, and at 3:50 A.M. he sent off Mrs. Putnam's Vega on its way to Los Angeles. A little over an hour later Turner left, followed forty-five minutes afterward by Wedell, Thaw, and Boardman. Boardman was all over the place on his takeoff, finishing his run in the grass about fifty feet to the left of the runway, obviously having practically no directional control over his Gee Bee. It lifted off at last, but he was back again in half an hour to see if something—anything—could be done to improve the handling. Probably the most sensible thing to do would have been to put a match to it. Boardman left again at six-twenty-five, just at sunrise. He would never see another one.

All the trouble began and, for some, ended at Indianapolis. Turner's 800 h.p. Wasp was gulping fuel at a ridiculous seventy-five gallons per hour—an awful lot more than he had expected. As a result he couldn't make it to Indianapolis nonstop. He put down at Columbus, Ohio, and wasted twenty

Russell Thaw puts the R-2 Gee Bee down at Indianapolis. After witnessing Boardman's accident, he very wisely decided not to continue. (UPI)

minutes looking for somebody to wake up. He took on fifty gallons and stormed off for Indianapolis again.

Lee Ghelbach's Wedell-Williams suffered a clogged fuel line almost within sight of Indianapolis Airport. He came down in a plowed field and slammed through a fence, ripping open a wing and bending the propeller. He was uninjured.

Russell Thaw got his Gee Bee all the way to Indianapolis, only to ground-loop it on landing. He was unhurt, but the R-2 was also out of the race now.

They were still looking over the damage when Boardman's R-1 arrived, making a safe if somewhat hot landing. He was fueled up again in short order, rolled out to the downwind end of the field, and began his take-off run. He seemed to have mastered his Gee Bee's directional instability now, as his run was dead straight along the runway, but the R-1 had one last vicious trick to pull. As Boardman was about fifty feet off, the R-1 started to roll to the left. Boardman fought to correct it, but his luck, at last, had run out. The Gee Bee smashed back onto the runway, upside-down, at 120 m.p.h. Boardman died two days later from multiple head injuries.

Roscoe Turner's arrival in Los Angeles as he won the Bendix Trophy couldn't have been staged better by Hollywood, which incidentally was Turner's home now. The opening parade of the National Air Races was just forming up at 12:29 P.M. as Turner flashed past the grandstands at Los Angeles Municipal Airport. He lofted his beautiful Wedell-Williams into a graceful *chandelle*, fell back on one wing, crabbed sideways over the fence at the edge of the field, and did a perfect three-pointe. Turner's time for the trip was 11 hours, 30 minutes, exactly. The new east-to-west transcontinental record and $5050 were his.

The crowd was just calming down again when Jimmy Wedell's "44" shot past, the only other finisher. Wedell's time was 11 hours, 58 minutes, 18 seconds. His share of the prize money, $2500.

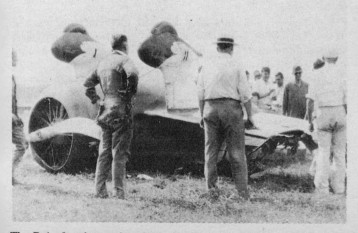

The R-1 after the crash at Indianapolis during the Bendix race. The Gee Bee had started to roll as it was lifted off. Boardman tried to stop it, to no avail, and it plowed back into the field upside down. (UPI)

The eventful, tragic race for the 1933 Bendix Trophy was over.

The qualifying runs for the Thompson this year were held on July 3, the day before the race. They were something of a disappointment this time, though. With the absence of the formidable Gee Bee's the contest was somewhat one-sided. The slim Wedell-Williams of Turner, Wedell and Ghelbach easily outran the field, although Ghelbach's "92," the slowest of the trio, wasn't all that much faster than Howard's incredible "Mike." Turner tried every way he knew to break 300 m.p.h., but his aircraft seemed to have lost a lot of steam in the last few days. It was only marginally faster than Wedell's aircraft, which was giving away some 359 cubic inches.

The final qualifying times posted, and the prize money, were:

Roscoe Turner	Wedell-Williams	280.274 m.p.h.	$1,125
Jimmy Wedell	Wedell-Williams	278.920 m.p.h.	$625
Lee Ghelbach	Wedell-Williams	251.930 m.p.h.	$375
Roy Minor	Howard "Mike"	241.612 m.p.h.	$250
Ray Moore	Keith Rider R-1	231.702 m.p.h.	$125

If the qualifying trials were dull, the race certainly wasn't. At the start Minor's tiny Howard outaccelerated everybody and began pulling away from the entire field going out to the scattering pylon! The crowd of fifty-five thousand was cheering the little white underdog for all it was worth, but "Mike's" moment of glory was about to end. As Minor whipped around the home pylon and onto his first lap, he was suddenly submerged in Wedell-Williams aircraft. Wedell took him on the outside, Turner from above, and Ghelbach went underneath as they thundered past. At the end of the first lap Turner's Wedell-Williams was pulling away from Wedell and Ghelbach at a tremendous rate. Whatever Turner's aircraft had lost before had certainly been found again.

Then, as they tore up the straight to the home pylon again ending their second lap, Wedell had taken the lead! The roar of the crowd was all but drowning the sound of the engines as they skimmed over the landscape and out onto their third lap. By the time they came home again Turner had taken over once more, and this time he stayed ahead, all the way home.

Ray Moore with his Keith Rider R-1 at Los Angeles. (UPI)

Turner beams as he carries off the Thompson Trophy immediately following the race. Because of a piffling rule infraction, they took it away from him a few hours later. (Wide World)

Turner covered the distance at an average of 241.031 m.p.h., and the reason for his dropping back on the second lap was soon explained. On his first lap he had cut the second pylon. He wasn't about to turn around and face the tail enders head-on, so he finished his first lap and then flew a high circle around the marker on his second lap, out of everybody's way—quite obviously the proper way to do it.

Mary Pickford was there to hand over the Trophy, and everybody was perfectly happy about the whole thing. Enter the villain, disguised as a National Aeronautical Association official. ''Turner didn't circle the pylon immediately before continuing the race. He is therefore disqualified.''

Turner tried an appeal, but the N.A.A. stood firm; if you want to recover a cut pylon, you've got to risk killing yourself, and someone else, to do it.

Roscoe Turner	Wedell-Williams	241.031 m.p.h.	Disqualified
Jimmy Wedell	Wedell-Williams	237.952 m.p.h.	$3,375
Lee Ghelbach	Wedell-Williams	224.947 m.p.h.	$1,875
Roy Minor	Howard "Mike"	199.870 m.p.h.	$1,125
George Hague	Keith Rider	183.206 m.p.h.	$750
Z. D. Granville	Gee Bee Model Y	173.079 m.p.h.	$375

There was another major air race held in 1933. This was at Curtiss-Reynolds Airport, near Chicago, in honor of the Century of Progress Exposition that was under way there.

There was a mixed bag of events held from September 1–4, but the big one was for the Frank Phillips Trophy and ten thousand dollars, held on the last day. Almost a carbon copy of the Thompson race held earlier that year, it was an unlimited free-for-all flown over twelve laps of an 8⅓-mile course (100 miles).

Jimmy Wedell took this one too, at 245.95 m.p.h., with Turner packing in on the eighth lap as his supercharger impeller started to chew itself up. Shortly after the race Wedell went after Doolittle's landplane record, and took it easily. His Wedell-Williams was now wearing the Wasp from the broken Gee Bee R-2, and the improvement was stunning. His best four runs averaged 304.98 m.p.h., with his fastest run at 316.

It was also in this race that young (twenty-five) Florence Klingensmith was killed when the fabric wing covering of her

The broken Gee Bee Model Y in which Florence Klingensmith was killed. (UPI)

Gee Bee Model Y began to tear away, sending her into a tree at over 200 m.p.h. It should be noted that this was not a Granville entry. In fact it was felt to be so overpowered (a monstrous 800 h.p. Wright Whirlwind) that the Granvilles would have nothing whatever to do with it.

It was about this time that the Gee Bee's began to get the reputation of being ''killers.'' In a way this was quite unfair, as their sports models which were sold to the public were among the most stable, dependable aircraft around in the 1930s.

Their racing models, as we shall see, were something else again . . .

The Bendix and Thompson Trophies— 1934

Early in 1934 Jimmy Wedell dropped a bombshell at the Pan American Air Races at New Orleans. During the preceding winter he had designed and built a magnificent new racing aircraft that was enough to strike fear into the hearts of every other racing pilot in the country. It had a full cantilever wing of remarkably thin section for the time, and was completely free of drag-inducing wire bracing. It also carried a fully retractable undercarriage that folded inward toward the fuselage. The resulting aircraft was a real bear (the U.S. Government later bought this design and designated it XP-34). Given the number "45," Wedell loafed around a 100-kilometer closed course at New Orleans at 264.703 m.p.h., setting a world record for a closed-circuit flight by a landplane, and Wedell didn't have it opened up all the way either, this being one of its first flights. Bearing in mind the fact that Turner's speed in the 1933 Thompson was "only" 241 m.p.h., it was pretty obvious that this was going to be a Wedell year, unless something unexpected happened. It did.

On June 24, Wedell was giving a flying lesson near his home field at Patterson, Louisiana. It is thought that the pupil panicked and froze at the controls. Jimmy Wedell was found dead in the wreckage.

And only a few weeks before, Zantford Granville had been making an approach for the airport at Spartanburg, South Carolina when at the last moment he saw workmen on the runway making repairs. He swerved to avoid them, lost control, and spun in from only seventy feet; not much of a distance to fall, but it was enough to kill him.

Benny Howard's magnificent "Mister Mulligan"—surely the most beautiful aircraft built anytime, anywhere. (Smithsonian Institution)

American sports aviation had suddenly lost two of its most powerful forces. But there were three new racing aircraft on the scene by midyear: a new one from Ben Howard, and another two by the reformed Granville, Miller & DeLackner organization.

Howard this time had surpassed himself. Working with Gordon Israel in a rented storefront on the ground floor of an apartment building near Chicago Municipal Airport, he had designed and constructed what was to become one of the most famous racing aircraft ever built. It was of course his magnificent "Mister Mulligan." With this superb aircraft Howard firmly established himself as one of the finest designers of private aircraft of all time.

Howard had again managed to get a measure of performance that seemed downright uncanny when looking at the bare figures. "Mister Mulligan" weighed over 2½ tons all up, and was powered by a P & W Wasp-SE which normally developed a mild 550 h.p., yet it would do 290 m.p.h. at sea level, and 312 m.p.h. at seventeen thousand feet—*with four passengers and luggage!*

As with all great conceptions, be they buildings or ballades, the science and art of this machine were inseparable, and inevitable. One wondered, after looking at it for the first time, why it hadn't always been done this way. The final proof of "Mister Mulligan's" integrity is that he looks just as modern today as he did in 1934.

One of the new Gee Bee's was the model "Q.E.D.," designed for the forthcoming London-Melbourne race. A much larger and more conventional aircraft than previous racing Gee Bee's, it mounted a P & W Wasp developing about 600 h.p. It had been built for Jacqueline Cochran.

The manners of this big green ship were a considerable improvement over its deadlier predecessors. Its only peculiarity was a tendency to suddenly drop out of the air from about 8–10 feet when the wing would stall on landing. It was a very strong aircraft, though, and seemed to cope with this kind of treatment quite well.

The other new Gee Bee was a hybrid, composed of the fuselage from Boardman's R-1 (with two feet added behind the cockpit), and the smaller, 1932 wing from R-2. Still carrying its P&W Hornet, the aircraft had been renamed "Intestinal Fortitude," a quality that its pilot would require in abundance.

With all these intriguing new aircraft about, the 1934 Bendix could have been the greatest ever. Instead, it was pretty nearly a flop. From the wide range of entries which had been prepared for this race, only two ended up finishing in it.

Lee Miles had intended to fly Haizlip's Wedell-Williams "92," but a leaky fuel system kept it out. Lieutenant Murry Dilley was to fly Claire Vance's flying wing, but he also remained in Burbank (Vance had died in a thunderstorm in the summer of '33 while flying his regular mail route). The Gee Bee hybrid "I.F.," with Roy Minor aboard, first jammed its starter and was then taxied into a ditch at the start. Lee Ghelbach in the Gee Bee "Q.E.D." got away at the start, only to be held up by a loose engine cowling which kept it from finishing within the time limit.

Roscoe Turner discovered a leak in his fuel tank at the start and had to withdraw. Turner had boosted his Wasp to nearly 1000 h.p. in an effort to stay in the picture this year. While on the way to Burbank, Howard's "Mister Mulligan" was forced down into a field near Hawthorne, Nevada. The aircraft was pretty badly beaten up and had to be withdrawn, though Howard was unhurt.

Ghelbach with Jacqueline Cochran's Gee Bee "Q.E.D." at Burbank. (UPI)

James Granger was to fly the marvelous new Keith Rider R-3. This was the only other aircraft around that looked like threatening the new Wedell-Williams "45," but not this year. As Granger was taking off, the tip of a propeller blade touched the ground, the aircraft flipped over, and Granger was killed.

As a result of all this attrition in the ranks, only Doug Davis, flying Wedell's "44," and Johnny Worthen in the formidable new Wedell-Williams "45" completed the Bendix this year. Davis got to Cleveland in 9 hours, 26 minutes, 41 seconds, having stopped at Goodland, Kansas and Lansing, Illinois. Davis' time was over an hour slower than Haizlip's 1932 mark, but it was enough to net him forty-five hundred dollars.

Worthen was surprised to discover he had overshot Cleveland, and he wasted half an hour finding it again. His time was 10 hours, 3 minutes, netting him twenty-five hundred dollars.

Vincent Bendix wasn't slow to realize that his race had laid an egg this year, and he quickly announced that an additional prize of thirty-five hundred dollars was now up for grabs. It would go to one of the remaining entrants in Los Angeles if he could break the transcontinental record. It was now held by Turner at 10 hours, 5 minutes, 38 seconds, set the previous September.

Turner got the message, and though the weather was terrible, he took off on what he later admitted was the most harrowing flight of his remarkable career. Nobody else bothered to try. Touching down for fuel at Albuquerque, Wichita, and St. Louis, Turner fought his Wedell-Williams all the way through violent storms, arriving at Cleveland in 8 hours, 25 minutes, and bringing the weather with him.

As he made a rather bumpy landing at Cleveland the skies opened up and a torrent of rain and heavy winds enveloped the field. Already some six minutes behind Haizlip's time, he would really have to go some now if he was to break his own record.

After a brief panic when it was discovered that the fuel filler wouldn't fit, his tanks were filled and he roared off down the field trailing a cloud of spray. The downpour was so heavy that he was out of sight before he had even left the ground. Luckily, the weather cleared up a few miles out of Cleveland, and the phenomenal speed of his aircraft was for once allowed to show itself. Turner flew this last leg flat out, the A.S.I. never showing less than 300 m.p.h.

When he touched down at Floyd Bennett he had broken his own transcontinental record by a scant 2 minutes, 39 seconds, his over-all time being 10 hours, 2 minutes, 59 seconds. It was midafternoon in New York as Turner managed a weak smile and a wave to the five-hundred-odd spectators who had waited for him. He went straight to the Half Moon Hotel nearby, flopped onto his bed, and didn't wake up again until the following afternoon.

There are certainly easier ways of making a living.

By the time the last day of the National Air Races had rolled around it had been made quite clear that Doug Davis was taking his racing very seriously this year. By swapping engines back and forth with Worthen's "45" he had collected $6390 so far, winning every event he entered. He now had his eye on the $4500 that came with a win in the Thompson, and he stood an awfully good chance of taking it. His qualifying speed was a hair faster than Wedell's landplane record, but not fast enough to be official. Turner's aircraft had once again turned temperamental, again refusing to get over the 300 m.p.h. hump.

Roscoe Turner alights after a disappointing qualifying run. His aircraft was not running well that day and was actually capable of well over 300 m.p.h. (UPI)

Designer Lawrence Brown alongside the new Brown B-2 shortly before its completion. It was flown in the Thompson by Roy Minor, securing second place. (UPI)

Doug Davis only moments before he became trapped in a high-speed stall. (UPI)

Doug Davis	Wedell-Williams "44"	306.215 m.p.h.	$875
Roscoe Turner	Wedell-Williams "2"	295.465 m.p.h.	$625
Johnny Worthen	Wedell-Williams "45"	292.141 m.p.h.	$375
Johnny Worthen	Wedell-Williams "92"	248.913 m.p.h.	$250
Roy Minor	Brown B-2 Special	243.145 m.p.h.	$125
Harold Neumann	Howard "Ike"	239.623 m.p.h.	$375
Roger Don Rae	Keith Rider R-1	235.336 m.p.h.	$225
Lee Miles	Miles-Atwood Spl.	233.44 m.p.h.	$150
Art Chester	Chester "Jeep"	229.715 m.p.h.	$75

There was a crowd of over sixty thousand on the afternoon of September 3 to watch the fifth race for the Thompson Trophy. They were also to witness a tragedy.

At the start Davis took the lead at once and began pulling away from the pack. Only Turner stayed with him, biding his time, about four hundred yards behind. About halfway through the twelve laps Turner made his bid . . . and discovered that he couldn't gain an inch on Davis, who was also opening up a bit more now.

On the eighth lap it happened. Davis, trying every way he knew to stay in front of Turner, misjudged his line at pylon No.2 and cut inside it. While still in the turn he threw his aircraft into a steep climb to go around again, and suddenly found himself helplessly caught in a high-speed stall. The Wedell-Williams slammed into the field near a clump of trees. It had to be cut apart before they could remove his body.

Turner continued on to win the Thompson, but there was no trace of the famous broad grin when the Trophy was handed over. Davis had been one of the most liked and respected men in American aviation.

1st	Roscoe Turner	Wedell-Williams	248.129 m.p.h.	$4,500
2nd	Roy Minor	Brown B-2 Special	214.929 m.p.h.	$2,500
3rd	Johnny Worthen	Wedell-Williams "92"	208.376 m.p.h.	$1,500
4th	Harold Neumann	Howard "Ike"	207.064 m.p.h.	$1,000
5th	Roger Don Rae	Keith Rider R-1	205.358 m.p.h.	$500
6th	Art Chester	Chester "Jeep"	191.597 m.p.h.	—

Lee Miles out on last lap.

Later in the year the top racing pilots in the country met to see what could be done about reducing the hazards of air racing. As a result, a technical subcommittee was formed, appointed by the pilots themselves, which would subject all new racing aircraft to a searching technical examination before they could be flown in competition.

All that was left of Wedell's ''44'' in which Davis lost his life. (UPI)

The Bendix and Thompson Trophies— 1935

The race for the 1935 Bendix Trophy was another that could have been the greatest ever. This time it almost made it. At any rate, the public wasn't likely to see another finish like this one for a long, long time.

Nine Cleveland-bound entries were lined up at Burbank on that early morning of August 30. Earl Ortman was making hurried, last-minute repairs to the Keith Rider R-3 which had pulled its cowling into the propeller on the first flight with its new 550 h.p. Wasp the day before.

Russell Thaw and Jacqueline Cochran had one Northrop "Gamma" each, and Roy Hunt was to fly his Lockheed "Orion." Royal Leonard was making final preparations to the big Gee Bee "Q.E.D." which, incidentally, had also tried several times to eat its cowling.

The Gee Bee R-½ hybrid, now called the "Spirit of Right," but otherwise unchanged, was to be flown by Cecil Allen.

The two big guns, Turner and Howard, were there, and on the face of it, it seemed that this was going to be a race between the two. Turner had now managed to get his highly stressed, 1000 h.p. Hornet to behave, and there was no doubt that his was the fastest aircraft there.

Outright speed, however, isn't everything, and Howard and Israel were counting on "Mulligan's" more dependable Wasp, and a few more little tricks they had been planning.

Amelia Earhart Putnam, with Paul Mantz, were last-minute entries with the big red "Vega."

Ortman had drawn the honors of being first away, and at

Cecil Allen's Gee Bee R-1/2 hybrid poses for photographers a few days before the start of the Bendix race. (UPI)

1:30 A.M. the R-3 thundered off on the first leg of the 1935 Bendix. By 3 A.M. everyone had gone but Cecil Allen in the R-½ Gee Bee. One wonders what must have been going through his mind as he shoved home the throttle and sent the Gee Bee streaking down the runway. No one will ever know. As he was halfway to the fence the aircraft suddenly swerved off line, making straight for the crowd of about ten thousand watching from the edge of the field, just as Boardman had done a few hours before the R-1 killed him. This time it didn't take so long.

Allen lifted it off at last, 150 yards before the fence, and charged into the thick fog that had begun rolling over the field. The flight lasted just two miles, ending in a potato patch east of Burbank. Nobody saw it happen. Two young boys discovered the smoking debris about twenty minutes after takeoff. Cecil Allen was dead, but the world, at last, was permanently rid of the infamous racing Gee Bee's.

Howard and Israel were naturally taking advantage of "Mister Mulligan's" exceptional range (about 1750 miles at cruise), and their first stop was at Kansas City, Missouri, after a long run of 1356 miles. They had also left the others struggling through the nasty weather down below, flying most of the way at 12,000–17,000 feet, using oxygen.

At precisely 1:41:16.3 P.M., "Mister Mulligan" swept past the timer's stand at Cleveland, the first Bendix entry to arrive, in the middle of another Cleveland downpour. There were only about twenty-five-hundred-diehard enthusiasts there, but they were certainly about to get their money's worth.

Howard and Israel got themselves as dry and as comfortable as possible and began waiting out the rest of the Bendix entries (all other events at Cleveland had been canceled for the day). The aircraft that had taken off before them were obviously not worrying them now, but those that had left later just might—and Turner was among them.

Turner's take-off time was announced over the public-address system (he had started about two hours after Howard and Israel), and he was reported to have made three stops, at Albuquerque, Wichita, and Indianapolis, and seemed to be making very good time. Howard and Israel waited.

The two-hour gap narrowed to ten minutes ... five minutes ... two ... one ... "Mister Mulligan's" crew was just beginning to relax now, when someone in the crowd shouted something, then all at once everybody was yelling, as a little gold Wedell-Williams dived out of a cloud and tore past the grandstands, forty feet over the field.

The watches were checked, starting times were verified, and the result was announced: Howard and Israel had won the Bendix by 23.5 seconds!

1st	Ben Howard	"Mister Mulligan"	8:33:16.3	$4,500
2nd	Roscoe Turner	Wedell-Williams	8:33:39.8	$2,500
3rd	Russell Thaw	Northrop Gamma	10:06:45	$1,500
4th	Roy Hunt	Lockheed Orion	11:41:03	$1,000
5th	Putnam-Mantz	Lockheed Vega	13:47:06	$500

There were three retirements from the Bendix this year, none of which were attended by damage or injury. Jacqueline Cochran's Northrop ran out of oil and was forced down at Kingman,

Earl Ortman established several new city-to-city records with the Keith Rider R-3 during 1935. This aircraft later evolved into the formidable Marcoux-Bomberg racer. (Wide World)

The end of the last flight of the Gee Bee racers in which Cecil Allen was killed. (UPI)

Howard and Israel taxi "Mister Mulligan" off the field after their arrival at Cleveland. Harold Neumann used the big white ship very effectively in the Thompson a few days later. (UPI)

Turner poses with his famous Wedell-Williams which was almost completely rebuilt early in 1935. (Wide World)

Arizona. Ortman's Keith Rider suffered a split fuel tank which grounded him at Kansas City, and Leonard's "Q.E.D." sprang a fuel leak at Wichita.

Howard and Israel had originally planned to fly all the way to New York and try for a new coast-to-coast record, but decided against it when they saw how bad the weather was at Cleveland. They had done enough for one day anyway, and Howard set about seeing what he could accomplish during the rest of the National Air Races. It turned out to be plenty.

For a start, "Mike" simply ran off with all three heats of the 550-cubic-inch Greve Trophy race on August 31 and September 1, brilliantly flown by Harold Neumann. This also netted a tidy forty-five hundred dollars for Howard, which looked awfully nice standing next to his forty-five-hundred-dollar Bendix winnings. He was soon to win a bit more.

All but two of the entries for this year's Thompson were fairly familiar to air racing fans. The two exceptions were a bulbous, Cyclone-powered amphibian designed and built by Major Alexis de Seversky which was to be flown by Lee Miles, and a weird but very hairy entry, "Bonzo," by Steve Wittman, a former barnstormer who was now an airport manager at Oshkosh, Wisconsin.

Wittman had started his racing back in 1926 in a Standard J-1, but his most notable successes had been with his little Cirrus-Hermes-engined "Chief Oshkosh" at the '32,'33, and '34 Nationals. The "Chief" had possessed all the qualities of its newer, bigger brother; it was clever, practical, stable, incredibly ugly, and surprisingly fast. But the competition was fast also, and though the "Chief" almost always finished in second, third, or fourth spot, outright wins were pretty scarce. The result was the amazing "Bonzo."

Back in 1934 Wittman had bought an 1145-cubic-inch Curtiss D-12 and had carefully rebuilt it, fitting high-compression pistons along the way.

Around this elderly but willing power plant Wittman proceeded to build the smallest possible airplane. "Bonzo" had a barn-door wing of twenty feet span, was twenty-three feet long, and looked like something wicked pilots might have to fly in the hereafter.

It was quite hot getting off and coming down, but was otherwise surprisingly well mannered. A few revisions had

Wittman's "Bonzo" flexes its muscles. (Smithsonian Institution)

Though it did not compete in the 1935 Bendix, Howard Hughes' very advanced R-1 set several new transcontinental records later in the year. (UPI)

been carried out, mostly to the cooling system, by the time the aircraft had arrived at Cleveland and it was now reasonably bug-free.

Turner's formidable Wedell-Williams was entered of course, as were Howard's "Mister Mulligan," to be flown by Greve-winner Harold Neumann, and "Mike," which would be flown by Joe Jacobson (who was now the owner of "Pete").

Weed C. Rogers had entered another Curtiss D-12-powered racer. Called the "Delgado Maid," it had been built by apprentices at the Delgado Trades School in New Orleans. Unfortunately, it was a few years behind the times.

Marion McKeen was to fly the Brown B-2 "Miss Los Angeles," formerly owned and flown by Roy Minor, and lastly, Roger Don Rae was to fly the Keith Rider R-1 "San Francisco I," now owned by Rudy Kling, a garage owner from Lemont, Illinois.

The qualifying speed for the Thompson was still 225 m.p.h., but this year this speed had to be exceeded over the actual Thompson course—the race was over ten fifteen-mile laps. Turner and Neumann were easily the fastest in these trials, with Wittman outrunning the rest of the field by a comfortable margin. This year all entries were to be started simultaneously, and as a result the pilots were thinking very hard about that first pylon. . . .

At the start Turner's gold Wedell-Williams tore away from the rest of the pack as though it had been shot off a catapult, whipped around the scattering pylon, and immediately became a dot on the horizon. "Mister Mulligan," with his weight working against him, was the last to get airborne. The "Delgado Maid" was left on the line puffing blue smoke.

Turner's lead was unassailable, but there was a great deal of argument about who was to occupy second place. For a while Rae held it by wringing every last erg of performance out of the Rider R-1, but Wittman's amazing "Bonzo" took over on the fourth lap, and slowly began to draw away.

"Mister Mulligan" was really on the move now. Starting from dead last, Neumann had been effortlessly picking them off one by one, and on the fifth lap he caught Rae and set out for Wittman. He caught him one lap later. "Mister Mulligan" was lapping in the 220's, and seemed pretty well set up to take second place. Once more, the Fates decided to step in . . .

Turner was on his last lap, possibly already musing over how he would spend the money, when his supercharger impeller disintegrated. In an instant everything was running in scalding oil—windshield, goggles, gloves, feet . . .

No one remembers seeing Neumann shoot past the finish line. Seventy-five thousand pairs of eyes were frozen on Turner's struggle with death eighty feet above the ground. Though he was wearing a parachute, he decided to ride it in and hope.

The smoke was all but suffocating him, but he somehow managed to see enough to find the airfield. The little ship came in fast—and *hard*. One big bounce . . . it started to roll over . . . he righted it again . . . another bounce . . . then another, and the crowd let out a roar the like of which had never been heard at Cleveland as the blackened Wedell-Williams, trailing smoke and dripping oil, slid to a stop.

1st	Harold Neumann	"Mister Mulligan"	220.194 m.p.h.	$6,750
2nd	Steve Wittman	Wittman "Bonzo"	218.686 m.p.h.	$3,750
3rd	Roger Don Rae	Keith Rider R-1	213.942 m.p.h.	$2,250
4th	Joe Jacobson	Howard "Mike"	209.103 m.p.h.	$1,500
5th	Lee Miles	Seversky Amphib.	193.594 m.p.h.	$375
6th	Marion McKeen	Brown B-2	188.859 m.p.h.	$375

Turner averaging 238 m.p.h. until breakdown.

As Turner was climbing out of his aircraft, a little unsteadily, someone in the crowd that was forming around him commented on his bad luck.

"What do you mean, bad luck?" he boomed, managing a grin. "Whenever something like that happens and you walk away from it, that's *good* luck!"

Amen.

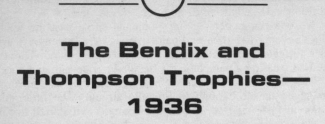

The Bendix and Thompson Trophies— 1936

Back on Christmas Day in 1934, Raymond Delmotte, the chief test pilot for the Caudron works in France, had finally broken Jimmy Wedell's landplane record after several failures, at 314.319 m.p.h. Then on May 19 of the following year Delmotte won the Coupe Deutsche de la Muerthe race, a closed (but very long) circuit event, at the very rapid pace of 275.724 m.p.h. Ordinarily, these speeds might not have caused too much of a stir, were it not for the fact that they were set by an aircraft with an engine under 488 cubic inches, virtually the same size as Ben Howard's little "Mike" and "Ike"! The aircraft was known as the Caudron C-460, and more was to be heard from it. Much more.

For two years now the organizers of the National Air Races had been pestering the French authorities to send a representative to compete in the major American closed-course events. They were about to get their wish . . . in spades.

This year the National Air Races were again held in Los Angeles, and the Bendix was flown once more from east to west, starting from Floyd Bennett Field, New York.

Even before the race was under way, the 1936 Bendix began to take its toll. Roscoe Turner, on his way from Glendale to New York in his venerable but still potent Wedell-Williams, had sudden engine failure over western New Mexico. He spotted a little Zuñi Indian farm and streaked toward it, the propeller now fanning uselessly in the slipstream. With his wheels hammering over the broken ground at about 85 m.p.h. and the tail beginning to settle, he was just on the verge of pulling off another incredible escape—when he hit the edge of a plowed field. The aircraft leaped into the air and cartwheeled end over end for fifty yards, finally slamming to a halt on its nose. Six inches behind Turner's head his beautiful Wedell-Williams was a mangled mess of fabric, wood, and steel. This time he didn't escape uninjured. When he got back to Los Angeles the next day his doctors diagnosed two cracked ribs and a very short temper.

The rest of the Bendix entries were lined up at Floyd Bennett Field shortly after midnight on the morning of September 4. There was quite a large entry this year, with a number of strictly commercial types making their first appearance in the Bendix.

There was the new Lockheed "Electra" of Amelia Earhart Putnam (this was the aircraft with which she would disappear over the Pacific the following year). Helen Richey would accompany Mrs. Putnam as her co-pilot.

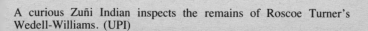

A curious Zuñi Indian inspects the remains of Roscoe Turner's Wedell-Williams. (UPI)

One of the new Douglas DC-2's (then America's largest commercial transport) was entered by George Pomeroy, who was also to serve as navigator. Louis Brewer was to do the flying.

A Vultee V1-A was to be flown by William Gulick and William B. Warner, and Joe Jacobson was to fly Gar Wood's Northrop "Gamma."

Louise Thaden and Blanche Noyes were to fly a G-17 staggerwing Beechcraft, which even in those days bore the stamp "classic" all over it. The last of the lady pilots, Laura Ingalls, was to fly her Lockheed "Orion."

Jacqueline Cochran twice broke the Northrop "Gamma" which she had planned to enter in the 1936 Bendix race—first damaging the undercarriage slightly which was soon repaired, and then a good deal more thoroughly (above) a few days later. (Wide World)

Benny and Maxine Howard with ''Mister Mulligan'' at Los Angeles
before the start of the race. (UPI)

There was one remaining entry, and everybody there knew it was going to win. Ben Howard and his wife Maxine were going to fly "Mister Mulligan." If anyone else did have thoughts of winning, they could only have been based on the hope that Howard and his wife might be delayed somehow. No one could possibly have wished for what actually happened.

The Gulick-Warner Vultee was the first away into the darkness at 1:37 A.M., followed at irregular intervals by the others. By 6 A.M. only Howard and Laura Ingalls were left at Floyd Bennett, "Mister Mulligan" thundering off at six-nine, followed by Miss Ingalls at six-sixteen.

There were only two retirements this year; one was almost comical, the other a near tragedy. Joe Jacobson, cheerfully flying Gar Wood's Northrop "Gamma" through the still morning air over Stafford, Kansas, suddenly heard a loud noise. When he looked around to see what it was, his aircraft was gone! It appears that an empty fuel tank in the fuselage exploded, blowing him out of the cockpit. He had been argued into borrowing a parachute back at the start. It saved his life.

The sun was directly overhead as Howard and his wife were settling into the second and last leg of their flight. Things were going very smoothly. They had left Kansas City a good half-hour ahead of Turner's transcontinental record. But as they were approaching the New Mexico-Arizona border, one of the deadliest of all mechanical failures struck—"Mister Mulligan" threw a propeller blade. The next moments were a seemingly eternal, violent, wrenching, jerking hell, ending at last with a mind-stopping jolt as the aircraft smashed into the hard New Mexico wilderness.

A few suspicious Navajo Indians cautiously made their way to the wreckage, but they were frightened away by the cries from inside. By the time help arrived they had been crushed underneath the huge engine for over four hours. Howard had suffered multiple compound fractures of both legs and a fractured skull. His wife also had both legs broken, but she was soon out of danger. One of Howard's legs was practically severed, and he was given a fifty-fifty chance to live. Miraculously, Howard pulled through in fine style, though it took him all of a year and a half to do it.

The first Bendix entrant to arrive at Los Angeles was the Gulick-Warner Vultee, but as they had also been the first to

The near-tragic end of "Mister Mulligan." (UPI)

leave New York, they would have to wait awhile before they knew where they stood. As it turned out they took third spot, humbled to that position by three of the ladies—much to everybody's surprise, excepting, of course, the ladies themselves.

1st	Thaden-Noyes	Beechcraft G-17	14:55:01	$7,000*
2nd	Laura Ingalls	Lockheed "Orion"	15:39:38	$2,500
3rd	Gulick-Warner	Vultee V1-A	15:45:25	$1,500
4th	Pomeroy-Brewer	Douglas DC-2	16:16:51	$1,000
5th	Putnam-Richey	Lockheed "Electra"	16:34:53†	$500

* Includes $2,500 for fastest flight by a woman pilot.
† Delayed several hours with engine trouble.

When Delmotte's magnificent Caudron C-460 arrived at Los Angeles, the aviation "experts" there could only gape at it in disbelief. It just seemed downright impossible that this rather large, unremarkable-looking aircraft with its undersized 488-cubic-inch engine could charge along at well over 300 m.p.h. (Delmotte had taken it in bursts to over 340.) Some of the aviation masterminds were quick to point out that although it

When Michel Detroyat's Caudron C-460 arrived at Los Angeles, the local aviation experts were mildly impressed, but not overly worried by its presence. Their attitude endured until Detroyat got his aircraft around the first lap of the qualifying trials. (Smithsonian Institution)

had flown a closed course at over 275 m.p.h., the course had been a very long one of 621 miles per lap. On the much tighter, fifteen-mile Greve and Thompson courses, they said, the French entry would soon be cut down to size.

Michel Detroyat, a brilliant French flier who had dazzled the crowds at the National Air Races over the last few years with his aerobatic displays in a Morane-Saulnier, had been appointed by the Caudron works to fly the C-460 this year at the Nationals.

All chatter about how ill-suited the French entry would be to the American course ended when Detroyat took the Caudron out to qualify for the Greve race. The Caudron's slowest lap was faster than anything that had ever gone around a closed circuit in the United States. The fastest lap, which was the only one that counted for qualification, was covered at 273.473 m.p.h. or about 1.25 m.p.h. short of its own record! So much for the experts.

A great wail of despair was heard from the pilots planning to fly in the Greve and Thompson races. It was suddenly so glaringly apparent that there wasn't anything in the world, let alone in the U.S.A., that could stay with this blue projectile, that a few of those present started looking around for excuses.

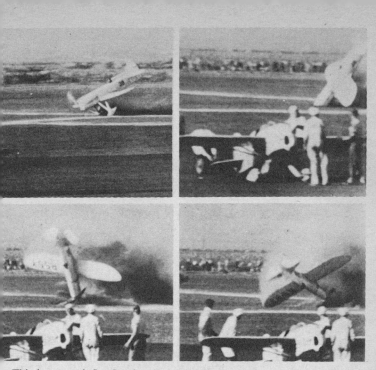

This just wasn't Joe Jacobson's year. After securing fifth place in the Greve race, "Mike's" undercarriage collapsed with the above result. Jacobson was unhurt. (UPI)

Some said that things would have been different if only Turner and Howard had been flying. Of course, they wouldn't have had a chance. Others grumbled that the C-460 had been financed, at vast cost, by the French Government. It just wasn't true. If there was any secret to it at all, it was simply that the Caudron C-460 was the most aerodynamically sophisticated thing in the air.

The ease with which Detroyat won the Greve and Thompson races was nothing short of embarrassing (it was strongly reminiscent of a certain Gordon Bennett race back in 1912). Earl Ortman put up a fine show in the Thompson, actually recording a speed that might have been good enough to win, but for the presence of a gifted Frenchman and his superb aircraft.

Jacobson standing beside his crippled Howard "Mike." (UPI)

Qualifying speeds for the 1936 Greve and Thompson races:

Michel Detroyat	Caudron C-460	273.473 m.p.h.	$450
Earl Ortman	Keith Rider R-3	258.90 m.p.h.	$250
Harold Neumann	Folkerts SK-2	230.061 m.p.h.	$450*
Art Chester	Chester "Jeep"	227.733 m.p.h.	$250*
Rudy Kling	Keith Rider R-1	226.444 m.p.h.	$250
David Elmendorf	Keith Rider R-5	224.551 m.p.h.	$150
Harold Neumann	Howard "Mike"	223.714 m.p.h.	$100
Roger Don Rae	Keith Rider R-4	218.155 m.p.h.	$50
Marion McKeen	Brown B-2	217.365 m.p.h.	—

*375-cubic-inch class.

GREVE TROPHY, SEPTEMBER 6

1st	Michel Detroyat	Caudron C-460	247.300 m.p.h.	$4,900
2nd	Harold Neumann	Folkerts SK-2	225.858 m.p.h.	$2,125
3rd	Art Chester	Chester "Jeep"	224.682 m.p.h.	$1,190
4th	Rudy Kling*	Keith Rider R-1	215.331 m.p.h.	$765
5th	Joe Jacobson*	Howard "Mike"	214.426 m.p.h.	$595
6th	Roger Don Rae	Keith Rider R-4	212.325 m.p.h.	$425

*Crashed upon landing. Unhurt.

1st	Michel Detroyat	Caudron C-460	264.261 m.p.h.*	$9,500
2nd	Earl Ortman	Keith Rider R-3	248.042 m.p.h.	$4,375
3rd	Roger Don Rae	Keith Rider R-4	236.559 m.p.h.	$2,450
4th	Harold Neumann	Folkerts SK-2	233.074 m.p.h.	$1,575
5th	Marion McKeen	Brown B-2	230.465 m.p.h.	$1,225
6th	Harry Crosby	Crosby Special	226.075 m.p.h.	$875

*Detroyat flew his first three laps at 280, 301, and 293 m.p.h.

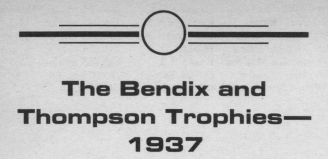

The Bendix and Thompson Trophies— 1937

Though the 1936 Nationals had been something less than a soothing balm to right-thinking, patriotic Americans, the 1937 year at least had all the earmarks of being the greatest one yet. Tantalizing aircraft were beginning to crop up all over.

Early in 1936 Roscoe Turner contracted with Lawrence Brown in Los Angeles for the construction of a new racing aircraft, to be built to Turner's design. It must have been clearer to Turner than to anyone else that his Wedell-Williams was becoming a flying fossil. Fast, to be sure, but no longer fast enough. Turner's approach was typical, direct, and went straight to the heart of the matter. Power. Great reverberating heaps of it, attached to an airframe crafted from the finest materials and built just large enough to keep everything under control.

Turner had gone the whole hog this time. The power plant was the biggest thing he could lay his hands on—a double-row 1830-cubic-inch Pratt&Whitney Twin Wasp Senior, conservatively rated by the factory at 1000 h.p. It wouldn't be too long before it was thumping out over twice that much. Just to play it safe, what was left of the old Wedell-Williams was being rebuilt by Matty Laird.

Steve Wittman had been blighted by bad luck at the 1936 Nationals. First the outlandish "Bonzo" caught fire (on the ground). Then the "Chief" was put out of the picture as it brushed against a parked aircraft and Wittman was forced out of a 100-mile opener. He was unhurt.

"Bonzo" had undergone considerable refinement since its

Roscoe Turner with his brand new "Meteor" which was built for him by Lawrence Brown and modified by "Matty" Laird. (Wide World)

Earl Ortman with the new Marcoux-Bomberg racer, a formidable new threat in the unlimited class. (Wide World)

first showing in 1935. Wittman's ingenious spring-steel landing gear (later to be seen everywhere when Cessna adopted it) had been fitted, and the cooling system had been revised again. Just to add the final touch, he had cut three feet off the wing. It was now down to seventeen feet!

In July of 1936, the Keith Rider R-3 was sold by the Rider-Clark association to Hal Marcoux, an employee of Douglas Aircraft at Santa Monica. Together with Jack Bomberg, a Douglas engineer, Marcoux proceeded to transform the R-3 from a merely promising design into a real threat in the unlimited class. The airframe was almost completely rebuilt and a new cowling was fitted for the '36 Nationals. Following Ortman's excellent showing in the Thompson, the R-3 was returned to Santa Monica. Its Wasp was removed and a double-row P&W Twin Wasp Junior was installed, driving a three-blade Hamilton propeller. The cockpit was moved back about a foot and the fuel capacity was increased to 240 gallons. A fresh all-over coat of black paint (with a silver cowl) finished off the new, and very impressive, Marcoux-Bomberg racer.

Also at the 1936 Nationals, Harold Neumann had startled quite a lot of people with his new Folkerts SK-2, lapping the slim little craft at 233 m.p.h., on 185 h.p.! Designed and built by Clayton Folkerts at Waterloo, Indiana, it was the first of two remarkable racing aircraft that were to burst brilliantly onto the scene, only to disappear almost at once. The other example was the SK-3, built for Rudy Kling, whose Keith Rider R-1 had been demolished in a landing accident at the end of the 1936 Greve race. This was a slightly larger aircraft than the SK-2, but it carried a 544-cubic-inch Menasco C6S boosted to over 400 h.p. If the amazing speed of the SK-2 was any guide, the performance of the SK-3 would be phenomenal.

Yes, 1937 was going to be quite a year.

If Turner had any hopes about his luck improving with his new aircraft, he was to abandon them right away. On September 2, the day before the start of the Bendix, a small welding job was being carried out on his magnificent new "Meteor" at Los Angeles. The welder was just finishing off the job when the center fuel tank exploded, blowing a great hole in the fuselage and puncturing Turner's Bendix plans for another year.

The remainder of the Bendix entries were lined up as usual at Union Air Terminal, Burbank, in the early hours of September 3. There were eight entries left now: seven men and the extraordinary Jacqueline Cochran.

If appearances meant anything, it looked as though the Bendix would now be a walkover for Earl Ortman and the Marcoux-Bomberg. This aircraft had a soul-stirring, brutal look to it now, and Ortman was confident he could average at least 340 m.p.h. for the trip.

Frank Fuller, heir to a sizable paint fortune and a well-known pilot on the West Coast, was to fly a stripped-down version of one of the new Seversky SEV-S2's (P-35), a dark horse with a very good chance. Frank Sinclair, a Seversky test pilot, was to fly an aircraft similar to Fuller's. Milo Burcham had entered a Lockheed Model 12, and Miss Cochran would be flying a staggerwing Beechcraft similar to the one which had won in '36. Another staggerwing Beech was to be flown by Bob Perlick.

A welcome surprise was Turner's old Wedell-Williams, rebuilt now and making its sixth try for the Bendix Trophy in the hands of Joe Mackey. Last was Eiler Sundorph in a Sundorph.

As the competitors took off one by one, some of them, particularly Ortman, had high hopes of beating Howard Hughes' transcontinental record of 7 hours, 28 minutes, 25 seconds, set January 19. But Ortman, who was certainly in a better position to do it than any of the others, was about to get another taste of the bad luck which was soon to become a steady diet.

On the last half of his run from Kansas City to Cleveland Ortman encountered bad weather, so he went above it. He went too high. Lacking oxygen equipment, he soon lost his bearings, sometime later discovering himself aimlessly touring over Lake Michigan. When he snapped out of it he reset his course for Cleveland and wound the Marcoux-Bomberg as tight as it would go. He got there just 11 minutes before the 6 P.M. deadline, but Fuller's Seversky had arrived nearly two hours sooner in elapsed time, finally breaking Jimmy Haizlip's durable 1932 Bendix time by a mild 25 minutes, 11 seconds. Nevertheless, Ortman took second place in this Bendix, a po-

Frank Fuller makes a low pass over the finish line at Cleveland, winning the 1937 Bendix race. (UPI)

sition he was getting to know much better than he would ever care to.

1st	Frank Fuller	Seversky SEV-S2	7:54:26	$13,000
2nd	Earl Ortman	Marcoux-Bomberg	9:49:21	$5,000
3rd	Jacqueline Cochran	Beechcraft	10:29:08	$5,500*
4th	Frank Sinclair	Seversky SEV-S2	11:02:33	$2,000
5th	Milo Burcham	Lockheed Model 12	11:03:58	$1,000

Perlick's Beechcraft undercarriage collapsed on takeoff.
Mackey's Wedell-Williams out at St. Louis. Oil leak.
*Includes $2,500 for fastest flight by a woman pilot.

When the unofficial qualifying trials opened in Cleveland on September 1, it was immediately obvious that the established pecking order was about to undergo some radical changes. For a start, Rudy Kling's new Folkerts SK-3 tore around the five-mile Greve course with one lap at 265.5 m.p.h., a whale of a lot faster than Detroyat had gone while winning the Greve the year before.

A couple of days later Wittman took his refined "Bonzo" out for a few trial laps and promptly had the timers blinking at their watches in astonishment. One lap was covered at just over 275 m.p.h.! "Bonzo" may have looked peculiar but it was going like the very devil now, and Wittman's handling of it left a lot of hard-nosed professional pilots pop-eyed and open-mouthed. Whatever mysterious incantation Wittman had breathed over "Bonzo," the little "Chief Oshkosh" must have overheard some of it. This little mouse with its dinky 363-cubic-inch Menasco won one of the opening races at 245.325 m.p.h.! As Turner once observed, it was enough to make any aeronautical engineer beat himself to death with his slide rule.

The official qualifying times for the Greve were somewhat slower, but no less interesting, as everyone seemed to be trying to outbamboozle everyone else.

Steve Wittman	Wittman "Chief"	224.685 m.p.h.	$900
Rudy Kling	Folkerts SK-3	223.104 m.p.h.	$900
Roger Don Rae	Folkerts SK-2	222.357 m.p.h.	$500
Art Chester	Chester "Jeep"	217.833 m.p.h.	$500
Marion McKeen	Brown B-2	192.014 m.p.h.	$300
Frank Haines	Haines "Mystery"	186.536 m.p.h.	$200

It wasn't too surprising that Kling ran off and hid from the rest of the Greve race. There was nothing really in the same league with the SK-3, and all Kling needed to do was fly it just fast enough to stay ahead of everyone else.

GREVE TROPHY RACE, SEPTEMBER 5

Rudy Kling	Folkerts SK-3	232.272 m.p.h.	$4,500
Steve Wittman	Wittman "Chief"*	231.990 m.p.h.	$2,500
Gus Gotch	Keith Rider R-4	231.593 m.p.h.	$1,500
Roger Don Rae	Folkerts SK-2	224.197 m.p.h.	$1,000
Marion McKeen	Brown B-2	223.644 m.p.h.	$500

*c-inch class.

Rudy Kling's superb Folkerts SK-3 posted a qualifying speed of 240.243 m.p.h. for the Thompson event, after easily outrunning the rest of the field in the Greve race. (Smithsonian Institution)

The 1937 Thompson Trophy race was, and is, probably the wildest, most thrilling air race ever held. Far from becoming a procession after the first lap, the race was fought over every inch of the two hundred miles, ending with a finish so close that for a while afterward nobody knew who had won.

By now Turner's new "Meteor" had been repaired, and arrived just in time to qualify for the Thompson. The official speeds again told a very interesting, if somewhat inscrutable, story:

Steve Wittman	Wittman "Bonzo"	259.108 m.p.h.	*
Roscoe Turner	Turner "Meteor"	258.903 m.p.h.	*
Earl Ortman	Marcoux-Bomberg	247.975 m.p.h.	$900
Joe Mackey	Wedell-Williams	247.029 m.p.h.	$500
Frank Sinclair	Seversky SEV-S2	242.082 m.p.h.	$900
Rudy Kling	Folkerts SK-3	240.243 m.p.h.	*
Ray Moore	Seversky SEV-S2†	231.565 m.p.h.	*
Gus Gotch	Keith Rider R-4	223.480 m.p.h.	$300
Roger Don Rae‡	Folkerts SK-2	174.474 m.p.h.	$500
Marion McKeen	Brown B-2	164.381 m.p.h.	$300

*No prize money for Group Three qualifying runs.
†Frank Fuller's Bendix-winning aircraft.
‡Undercarriage collapsed at end of Greve race.

There was a refreshing feeling of tenseness in the air as the time for the Thompson approached. It was a feeling that hadn't been too noticeable in the last few years, and possibly had never again reached the pitch of the 1932 race when Doolittle flew that Gee Bee. The public certainly sensed it. Well over one hundred thousand spectators showed up on the last afternoon to see this Thompson race, and they weren't likely to forget it in a hurry.

As the nine aircraft were lined up in front of the stands for the start, they presented a stirring spectacle of color and courage; perhaps something akin to the atmosphere that must have preceded a medieval joust. Brave and skillful men, about to meet in the world's most demanding sport. Once having tasted of it, any other pastime must have seemed almost inexpressibly foolish.

The pilots began to climb aboard, trying and failing to look calm. Nine engines were started up, and they waited out the last few seconds (they unanimously agreed that this was the worst time of all).

The starter's flag snapped the tenseness, and McKeen's lightweight little Brown pulled away from the field as they moved off the line. But before McKeen had reached the scattering pylon he had been swamped by the jockeying, thundering pack. Turner skidded violently in the first turn to avoid ramming another aircraft and Wittman grabbed the lead. At the end of the first lap "Bonzo" led the field past the stands followed by Ortman, Sinclair, and Mackey, with Turner closing up last. Kling had some trouble getting his gear up and was the last man to end his first tour.

The second lap saw Wittman even farther ahead, lapping in the 250's. Sinclair had moved his Seversky into second place, and Turner and Mackey were fighting wing-to-wing for third. On the next round Ortman got by both Turner and Mackey to take third spot, Turner sliding in behind him. On the fourth round Wittman lapped tail-ender Gotch, and Kling had moved up to sixth place, ahead of Moore's Seversky and McKeen.

Turner began pressing Ortman on his sixth lap, in the process both of them getting past Sinclair, Turner slipping into second place on his seventh lap.

At eight laps the order was Wittman (miles ahead now), Turner, Ortman, Sinclair, and Kling steadily working his way

Steve Wittman standing next to his astonishing "Bonzo." (Smithsonian Institution)

up, followed by Mackey, Moore, McKeen, and Gotch.

Turner now began pouring on the coal, and set out after Wittman, who promptly began to lap at 265 m.p.h.! He was so far ahead now (nearly half a lap) that there was little that could be done about it. Turner now slowly began to draw away from Ortman, but he was making no impression at all on the amazing "Bonzo."

Mackey and McKeen retired on the fifteenth round, the order now being Wittman, Turner, Ortman, Kling, Sinclair, Moore, and Gotch. It looked as though the race was all but decided now, and the crowd was at last getting a chance to catch its breath when, at the end of the seventeenth lap Wittman suddenly swung wide of the course and started clawing for altitude. Everyone thought he was preparing to jump, but after throttling back (vibration) he decided to continue.

At the rate Turner and Ortman had been going they were past Wittman within a few seconds, and now Kling was suddenly coming up—fast! On the next-to-last lap Turner had one of his attacks of pylonitis. Blinded by the sun on the oil-streaked windshield, he thought he had missed the last turn on the backstretch. There was nothing else he could do. He pulled up, handed over the lead to Ortman, and went back for the pylon.

Ortman had only one lap to go now to win. To make sure

he finished, he throttled back a bit and began coasting toward the finish line and the 1937 Thompson Trophy.

Kling had been waiting for him to do something like that. Flying in Ortman's blind spot, high and about a hundred feet behind, Kling shoved everything into the firewall and put the Folkerts into a shallow dive down the homestretch . . .

The crowd could see what was about to happen, but poor Ortman couldn't. The first he knew about it was when he saw a cream-and-black object shoot past him overhead as he crossed the line.

Rudy Kling won the Thompson Trophy by 0.052 m.p.h.!

THOMPSON TROPHY RACE, SEPTEMBER 6

1st	Rudy Kling	Folkerts SK-3	256.910 m.p.h.	$9,000
2nd	Earl Ortman	Marcoux-Bomberg	256.858 m.p.h.	$5,000
3rd	Roscoe Turner	Turner "Meteor"	253.802 m.p.h.	$3,000
4th	Frank Sinclair	Seversky SEV-S2	252.360 m.p.h.	$2,000
5th	Steve Wittman	Wittman "Bonzo"	250.108 m.p.h.	$1,000
6th	Ray Moore	Seversky SEV-S2	238.411 m.p.h.	$300
7th	Gus Gotch	Keith Rider R-4	217.810 m.p.h.	$250

As if all this hadn't been enough, it was announced shortly after the race that Turner had been well outside that pylon the first time around. He had given up a certain win for nothing.

As a measure of the man, someone asked Turner afterward if he wanted to comment on the race. His only remark, with a shrug, "I just didn't fly it very well."

The Bendix and Thompson Trophies— 1938

Well before the 1938 Nationals, there were two incidents which totally upset the never-too-dependable predictions of aviation's crystal-gazers. Rudy Kling, whose Folkerts SK-3 had won everything at the 1937 races but the organizers' shirts, was killed during a somewhat minor race at Miami December 3. Frank Haines, flying his "Mystery S-3," died with him as they charged into the first turn at the scattering pylon.

Then on May 30, Earl Ortman took on Roscoe Turner, 1250 h.p. Meteor and all, and soundly trounced The Master in a 150-mile closed-course event at the Pacific International Air Races at Oakland, California. The Marcoux-Bomberg was going now as it had never gone before. Ortman won this race at 265.539 m.p.h., setting up a new United States closed-course record over a tight 8⅓-mile course. Turner followed Ortman at 262.402 m.p.h.

Armchair handicappers were given another startling new factor to puzzle over at the Oakland races. A young newcomer named Tony LeVier astounded everyone by fighting wing-to-wing with Turner for the first five laps before dropping oil pressure forced him to slow up, finishing at 260.762 m.p.h. LeVier's mount was the seemingly harmless Schoenfeldt-Rider R-4 "Firecracker" that Gus Gotch had campaigned in 1937. LeVier had cleaned the ship up a bit, but had spent months working over the Menasco C6S4 and finding a propeller that satisfied him. Whether he was completely happy with the result was doubtful, but there was no doubt that a lot of other people were decidedly unhappy about it. LeVier was about to arrive, and somebody was going to have to move over.

The field for the Bendix race this year was the biggest one ever, and of the eleven entries posted, ten started. The one dropout was the remarkable Bernarr Macfadden, then a mere seventy years old, who bent his Northrop "Gamma" two days before the race.

There were two new rules this year, both of them very sound and welcome. All pilots were now required to have an instrument rating and would have to carry radio equipment. Also, no aircraft entering the Bendix would now be eligible for the closed-course events in Cleveland. Temperamental, highly strung closed-course racers had no more business being in a cross-country race than a twenty-seven-seat transport had in the Thompson, and the way was now clear to promote the development of aircraft which could do one thing well, rather than try, and fail, to be all things to all men.

As they lined up at Burbank on the evening of September 2, the entries were as follows:

Frank Fuller's Seversky SEV-S2—the 1937 winner.

Jacqueline Cochran's Seversky SEV-S2—in which Major de Seversky had set a new east-to-west record of 10 hours, 3 minutes, 7 seconds just two days before.

Max Constant, flying Miss Cochran's staggerwing Beechcraft.

Ross Hadley's staggerwing Beechcraft, with Al Larry as co-pilot.

Bob Perlick's staggerwing Beechcraft, which had collapsed under him on takeoff at the start of the previous year's Bendix.

George Armistead in the Gee Bee "Q.E.D.," now fitted with a Hornet and still looking for a win.

Lee Ghelbach's Wedell-Williams—Haizlip's old "92," now called "The Utican."

Paul Mantz's Lockheed "Orion"—Mantz was now a busy Hollywood stunt pilot.

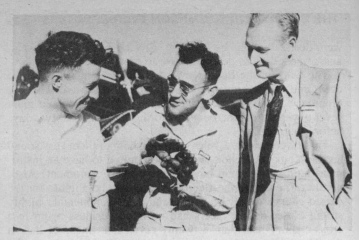

Steve Wittman does a little hangar flying at the Miami races the following December while Rudy Kling and Frank Haines look on. Both Kling and Haines were killed the following day. (UPI)

The shattered wreckage of Rudy Kling's Folkerts at Miami. (UPI)

Frank Cordova's Bellanca trimotor—very fast but unreliable.

John Hinchey's Spartan Executive, with Charles LaJatte as co-pilot.

There were some forty thousand determined night-owls gathered around the airfield to watch the start of the eighth race for the Bendix Trophy (they caused a traffic jam, incidentally, that veteran Los Angeles police still talk about).

Hadley's Beechcraft was the first to leave at 1:47 A.M., followed by Constant, Miss Cochran, and the rest at irregular intervals, the last man away being Cordova at 5:43 A.M.

This Bendix was the most incident-free in the history of the event. There is really very little to report, except that Miss Cochran outran and outnavigated all the men, to win by 23 minutes, 2 seconds from Frank Fuller. Miss Cochran had flown the entire distance to Floyd Bennett Field at twenty thousand feet and above, on instruments all the way, getting only one brief, meaningless peek at the ground as she passed over Ohio. It was a beautifully executed flight, though somewhat tarnished by a patronizing popular press who were, as ever, hard put to disguise their astonishment at a woman doing anything of significance with an aircraft. This, of course, was before the days of round-the-world flights by housewives.

BENDIX TROPHY, SEPTEMBER 3

1st	Jacqueline Cochran	Seversky SEV-S2	8:10:31	$14,500
2nd	Frank Fuller	Seversky SEV-S2	8:33:29	$5,800
3rd	Paul Mantz	Lockheed "Orion"	9:36:25	$3,000
4th	Max Constant	Beechcraft	10:14:39	$2,000
5th	Ross Hadley	Beechcraft	11:13:46	$1,000
6th	John Hinchey	Spartan	11:30:27	—

George Armistead—out at Winslow, Arizona.
Bob Perlick—out at Wood River, Illinois.
Frank Cordova—out at Bloomington, Illinois.
Lee Ghelbach—out at Kansas City.

Jacqueline Cochran taxis off the runway at Floyd Bennett after setting a new transcontinental record and in the process winning the 1938 Bendix. (UPI)

The qualifying trials for the Greve and Thompson races began on August 31, several days before the opening of the Nationals. The speed requirements were still 200 and 225 m.p.h., but entrants were now allowed three tries in individual, two-lap dashes, the average of both laps being recorded as the official qualifying mark.

Turner, Ortman, and Mackey were the first to qualify, early in the morning of the first day. Leigh Wade, in Hawks' "Time Flies," tried a few hours later but could only manage 213.523 m.p.h. in a very bad wind that had sprung up. Jacobson, LeVier, and Chester also tried and failed for assorted reasons. Later on Roger Don Rae qualified the new Keith Rider R-6 and the Folkerts SK-4 for Jacobson. The organizers eventually decided that they didn't approve of this, so Jacobson had to qualify them himself afterward.

Joe Mackey with Turner's rebuilt Wedell-Williams. This aircraft is now in the Frederick C. Crawford Auto-Aviation Museum in Cleveland. (UPI)

Harry Crosby's exquisite CR-4. (UPI)

Leigh Wade with the rebuilt "Time Flies" which Frank Hawks had been using for the past two years. This was the last Granville-designed aircraft. (UPI)

			Greve	Thompson
Roscoe Turner	Turner "Meteor"	281.250 m.p.h.		*
Steve Wittman	Wittman "Bonzo"	277.780 m.p.h.		*
Earl Ortman	Marcoux-Bomberg	270.437 m.p.h.		*
Art Chester	Chester "Goon"	268.456 m.p.h.	*	*
Leigh Wade	Hawks "Time Flies"	264.317 m.p.h.		*
Joe Mackey	Wedell-Williams	261.488 m.p.h.		*
Tony LeVier	Rider "Firecracker"	259.740 m.p.h.	*	*
Joe Jacobson	Folkerts SK-4	251.748 m.p.h.	*	*
Harry Crosby	Crosby CR-4	239.680 m.p.h.	*	*
Joe Jacobson	Keith Rider R-6	230.621 m.p.h.	*	*
George Dory	Keith Rider R-2	214.413 m.p.h.	*	

The Greve was the one that stopped the show this year. Six aircraft were lined up at the start, but it was already obvious that the race was going to be between Chester's sleek new

"Goon" and LeVier's "Firecracker" (Jacobson withdrew the SK-4 after detecting incipient wing flutter).

At the drop of the flag Chester and LeVier charged away from the line and were already around the scattering pylon before most of the others were airborne. As they ended their first lap Chester was about five lengths ahead, but not for long. At five laps LeVier was holding a slim, twenty-foot lead over Chester, both of them going at such a rate that they had already lapped the entire field. Chester grabbed the lead on the eighth, only to lose it again for the next three laps. Chester got the lead once more on the twelfth, and this time looked as though he was going to stay there, but on the fifteenth his luck ran out. Oil began spraying from the propeller hub, smearing the windshield, and almost at once he cut a pylon. Chester snapped around and shot back, letting LeVier through to what now seemed a certain win.

But Chester wasn't giving up so easily. With every gauge over the limit, he stormed off again after LeVier, now twenty-two seconds ahead. On the sixteenth lap Chester had cut it down to seventeen seconds . . . on the seventeenth eleven seconds . . . on the eighteenth five seconds, and on the nineteenth lap he caught him. By now the oil leak was so bad that Chester was flying more by guesswork than by sight, and he was forced to fly the last few corners fairly wide. Instantly LeVier sliced by on the inside and won the Greve Trophy by half a mile per hour!

GREVE TROPHY, SEPTEMBER 4

1st	Tony LeVier	Rider "Firecracker"	250.880 m.p.h.	$12,500
2nd	Art Chester	Chester "Goon"	250.416 m.p.h.	$5,000
3rd	Joe Jacobson	Keith Rider R-6	218.278 m.p.h.	$2,000
4th	Earl Ortman	Keith Rider R-5	192.503 m.p.h.	$1,000

Harry Crosby—out on fourteenth lap, exhaust manifold.
George Dory—out on twelfth lap, engine.

During the race, George Dory's Keith Rider R-2 (once flown by George Hague and Ortman, now called the Bushev McGrew Special) threw a rod at low altitude. Dory tried to put it down in a dead-end street. He was taken to a nearby hospital, seriously injured.

Steve Wittman with his astonishing "Bonzo." (UPI)

Tony Levier with the formidable new "Firecracker." (UPI)

The Thompson race was almost an anticlimax after the cliff-hanging Greve event, although for a time it appeared there was going to be more at stake than a trophy. It seems that one of the Thompson pilots had bragged to his girl that he was going to crowd Turner at a corner and drive him into a pylon. Turner got wind of it just before the race. Not knowing who would brag about being so stupid, Turner rounded up all the pilots and made a little speech, most of which cannot be printed here.

The result of the sermon was that Turner was left very much alone so he could deal with Ortman's Marcoux-Bomberg—which was not all that easy to do. Turner had a pretty hard time of it until his rival used up all his oil on the thirteenth lap. Roscoe went on to set a new record for the Thompson at 283.419 m.p.h., becoming the first man to win the Trophy twice.

As one of the race officials observed afterward, "The Thompson couldn't have turned out more popularly if it had been rigged."

THOMPSON TROPHY, SEPTEMBER 5

1st	Roscoe Turner	Turner "Meteor"	283.419 m.p.h.	$22,000
2nd	Earl Ortman	Marcoux-Bomberg	269.718 m.p.h.	$9,000
3rd	Steve Wittman	Wittman "Bonzo"	259.187 m.p.h.	$4,500
4th	Leigh Wade	Hawks "Time Flies"	249.842 m.p.h.	$2,500
5th	Joe Mackey	Wedell-Williams	249.628 m.p.h.	$1,800
6th	Joe Jacobson	Keith Rider R-6	214.570 m.p.h.	$1,400
	Art Chester—completed twenty laps, propeller throwing oil.			$600
	Harry Crosby—started late, completed ten laps.			

Ortman with the final version of the Marcoux-Bomberg at Cleveland on the day before the races opened. (UPI)

Turner follows his "Meteor" back to the hangar after setting up the fastest qualifying time over two laps at 281.250 m.p.h. (Smithsonian Institution)

The Bendix and Thompson Trophies— 1939

During the summer of 1939 most of the Americans who bothered to think about it realized that the daily deteriorating situation in Europe must inevitably upset a great many aspects of life in the United States. Anyone with half an eye could see that it would only be a matter of time. The National Air Races went off as scheduled—and Europe exploded into war right in the middle of it. It was suddenly clear that an era was about to die.

The Bendix race this year was just too successful for its own good. Everybody who started, finished, and even though a new Bendix record was set the classic had somehow lost something over the last few years. Even the once-enthusiastic aviation journalists weren't bothering to disguise their boredom any more. Perhaps it was because regularly scheduled transcontinental flights were commonplace now. Or it might have been due to the absence of the "Mister Mulligans," the Wedell-Williamses, the Gee Bees, the Super Solutions—the romantic, almost other-worldly aircraft that had gripped the public's attention wherever they went. Whatever the reason, Frank Fuller's winning Bendix flight in his Seversky caused so little excitement as to be barely noticeable.

The race from San Francisco to Floyd Bennett was totally uneventful, except for Jacqueline Cochran's withdrawal at the start. She had tried several times to get off in a pea-soup fog, eventually giving up when she could barely see the runway.

Frank Fuller puts down his Seversky SEV-S2 after an uneventful record-breaking flight from San Francisco to Floyd Bennett in seven hours, fourteen minutes and nineteen seconds. (UPI)

BENDIX TROPHY, SEPTEMBER 2

1st	Frank Fuller	Seversky SEV-S2	7:14:19	$12,500
2nd	Arthur Bussey	Bellanca tri-motor	8:21:08	$5,800
3rd	Paul Mantz	Lockhead "Orion"	8:41:38	$3,000
4th	Max Constant	Beechcraft	8:49:33	$2,700
5th	Arlene Davis	Spartan	10:22:25	—
6th	William Maycock	Lockheed "Vega"	10:54:32	—

Once again the qualifying trials began several days before the official opening of the Nationals in Cleveland. The speed requirements had been boosted again this year. The Greve was up to 220 m.p.h., and the admission charge into the Thompson had been raised to 240 m.p.h.

The practice sessions opened on August 27, and they had no sooner begun when another man died. Delbert Bush, flying the Folkerts SK-4 that Jacobson had withdrawn the year before, was caught off guard by engine failure at low altitude near the airfield. The aircraft immediately dropped like a tombstone, tearing into a small stand of trees nearby.

On the following day Turner issued formal warning of his intentions. His Twin Wasp was now pounding out over 2000 h.p., and no one was more surprised about it than Pratt &

Whitney. Turner set up an official two-lap average of 297.767 m.p.h., cut a few unofficial laps over 300, getting his "Meteor" into the 350's along the straights. LeVier and Mackey also qualified on the same day, the little "Firecracker" once more putting up a speed that was hard to believe: 277.163 m.p.h. Mackey got Turner's old Wedell-Williams around at 251.221 m.p.h. Though clearly outclassed, it was faster now than it had ever been.

Three days later, on August 31, Wittman, Ortman, and Leland Williams (in McKeen's Brown B-2) qualified, several others giving up after failing to meet the speed requirements. As before, entrants were allowed three tries at qualifying, so they weren't too unhappy about it.

On September 1 Chester qualified his "Goon," but the carnival atmosphere had all but evaporated that morning with the news from across the Atlantic: Germany had invaded Poland.

By the close of the qualifying runs on the afternoon of the Greve race, the final speeds stood as follows:

			Greve	Thompson
Roscoe Turner	Turner "Meteor"	297.767 m.p.h.		*
Tony LeVier	Rider "Firecracker"	277.163 m.p.h.	*	*
Steve Wittman	Wittman "Bonzo"	273.764 m.p.h.		*
Art Chester	Chester "Goon"	268.857 m.p.h.	*	*
Harry Crosby	Crosby CR-4	263.158 m.p.h.	*	*
Joe Mackey	Wedell-Williams	251.221 m.p.h.		*
Earl Ortman	Marcoux-Bomberg	244.565 m.p.h.		*
George Byars	Keith Rider R-6	234.834 m.p.h.	*	
Leland Williams	Brown B-2	228.137 m.p.h.	*	

Only four aircraft flew in the Greve, Byars' Rider R-6 being plagued by a moody Menasco. LeVier, Chester, Crosby, and Williams left the line in a tight little group, and before sixty seconds had passed Williams was dead. He seemed to be somewhat unsteady from the moment he left the ground. The little Brown stalled at the scattering pylon and bored into the ground, killing its pilot instantly.

To no one's surprise LeVier charged into the lead and stayed

Potentially an extremely fast aircraft, this Folkerts SK-4 was totally destroyed and its pilot Delbert Bush was killed when the engine stalled at low altitude on the first day of the practice trials at Cleveland. (UPI)

Hal Marcoux and Earl Ortman, two of the three driving forces behind the Marcoux-Bomberg racer, are interviewed by the press. (UPI)

Art Chester with his superb Menasco-powered "Goon." Along with LeVier's "Firecracker," these were the fastest aircraft in the world in their displacement class. (UPI)

there for the first eleven laps. His engine then began to miss and started losing power rapidly. LeVier put down fast while he still had some left. Chester inherited the lead and the one remaining entry, Crosby, was flagged down at thirteen laps after failing to get his wheels up. As a result, Chester finished the Greve by himself, but without easing up in the slightest, setting a record speed for the event.

Leland Williams tows Marion McKeen's Brown B-2 off the field after qualifying it at 228.137 m.p.h. He was killed on the opening lap of the Greve race. (UPI)

Leland Williams' crash. One mistake is all it takes. (UPI)

GREVE TROPHY, SEPTEMBER 3

1st	Art Chester	Chester "Goon"	263.390 m.p.h.	$9,000
2nd	Tony LeVier	Rider "Firecracker"	lapped at 271 m.p.h.	$1,320
3rd	Harry Crosby	Crosby CR-4	lapped at 164 m.p.h.	$1,000

Though the climax of the Greve race may have been dull, there was plenty to occupy the minds of the spectators. Britain and France had declared war on Germany that morning, and occasional announcements were made over the public-address system as more news arrived from overseas. There were quite a few suitcase-size portable radios in the stands, each one drawing around it a cheerless, quiet little group.

The race for the Thompson Trophy was postponed by another torrential rainstorm September 4 (Labor Day), which soaked to the skin some one hundred thousand spectators. The following day was beautiful, but this was little consolation to those who had to get back to work, many of whom had traveled halfway across the country to see the Greve and Thompson. Nonetheless a sizable crowd of about sixty thousand turned up to watch on that Tuesday afternoon.

On the line were the seven Thompson entries: Turner's silver "Meteor," LeVier's yellow "Firecracker," Ortman's Marcoux-Bomberg now in yellow and black, Wittman's red "Bonzo," Chester's pale cream "Goon," Crosby's polished aluminum CR-4, and Turner's Wedell-Williams in the hands of Joe Mackey, as ever in its coat of dazzling gold. It was an unforgettable sight.

When the flag dropped Wittman won the drag race off the line and "Bonzo" led the field around the scattering pylon and onto the first lap. As they came around again Wittman still led, with Mackey's Wedell-Williams holding onto an amazing second place. They were both on borrowed time, though, as LeVier was slashing his way up, and finally took over the lead on the fifth lap.

But what was Turner doing dawdling about in last place? The word soon came through—he had cut another pylon! It was almost as though he had realized that it was expected of him, particularly since he had forgotten to cut one in 1938.

Roscoe Turner in the process of winning the Thompson Trophy for the third time. Turner's ''Meteor'' was a good deal faster than most of the world's combat aircraft at the start of World War II. (Wide World)

Fred Crawford hands over the Thompson Trophy to the immortal Roscoe Turner for the third and last time. (Wide World)

Once Turner had found the missing pylon, he proceeded to show the sixty thousand spectators, and the six other pilots, just why he had dominated air racing in the United States for so long.

Flying the race of his life, Turner had the spectators falling off their seats as they watched him overhaul the field one by one, lapping at over 300 m.p.h. and streaking past the stands not too far under 400. It looked almost absurdly easy. By the ninth lap he had taken over the lead. He eased up a bit afterward, but still managed to lap everybody *again* before the end.

Roscoe Turner had won the Thompson Trophy for the third and last time.

THOMPSON TROPHY, SEPTEMBER 5

1st	Roscoe Turner	Turner "Meteor"	282.536 m.p.h.	$16,000
2nd	Tony LeVier	Rider "Firecracker"	272.538 m.p.h.	$8,000
3rd	Earl Ortman	Marcoux-Bomberg	254.435 m.p.h.	$4,000
4th	Harry Crosby	Crosby CR-4	244.522 m.p.h.	$2,500
5th	Steve Wittman	Wittman "Bonzo"	241.361 m.p.h.	$1,500
6th	Joe Mackey	Wedell-Williams	232.926 m.p.h.	$1,000

Art Chester—out after seventeen laps.

As soon as he was down, Turner made the announcement that his closest friends knew he was to make. He was retiring from air racing—for good. He was getting old, he said, though it certainly hadn't been apparent a few minutes before. He planned to open an air service flying school at Indianapolis, and he did precisely that. As a result, several hundred American pilots going into combat a few years later had one huge psychological advantage over the enemy: Roscoe Turner had taught them to fly.

Epilogue

Few realized it at the time, having suddenly more urgent matters to think about, but that last Thompson Trophy race marked the abrupt end of an incredibly exciting, ceaselessly fascinating era in the history of flight.

As historical eras go, the thirty-one years between that first Gordon Bennett at Rheims and the last Thompson before the war are but a few moments in history. But during that brief span man finally mastered the last of the elements that had resisted him. It was an incredibly exciting era, rich with both comedy and tragedy: Lefebvre being fined for doing too well what was expected of him, Boardman's luck finally running out though his courage never did, the Royal Aero Club losing its hatrack, Agello's magnificent record. . . . Here was a group of men who had discovered the most demanding pastime imaginable, and went at it with a vengeance—not really so much in the cause of progress, but simply because they had to. As long as there are men like this, there must be hope for the world after all.

To your health, gentlemen! May you never be forgotten.

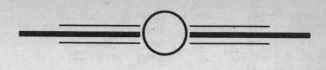

Index

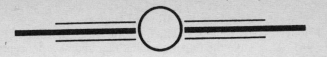

A Note About The Bantam Air & Space Series

This is the era of flight—the century which has seen man soar, not only into the skies of Earth but beyond the gravity of his home planet and out into the blank void of space. An incredible accomplishment achieved in an incredibly short time.

How did it happen?

The AIR & SPACE series is dedicated to the men and women who brought this fantastic accomplishment about, often at the cost of their lives—a library of books which will tell the grand story of man's indomitable determination to seek the new, to explore the farthest frontier.

The driving theme of the series is the skill of *piloting*, for without this, not even the first step would have been possible. Like the Wright brothers and those who, for some 35 years, followed in their erratic flight path, the early flyers had to be designer, engineer and inventor. Of necessity, they were the pilots of the crazy machines they dreamt up and strung together.

Even when the technology became slightly more sophisticated, and piloting became a separate skill, the quality of a flyer's ability remained rooted in a sound working knowledge of his machine. World War I, with its spurt of development in aircraft, made little change in the role of the flyer who remained, basically, pilot-navigator-engineer.

Various individuals, like Charles Lindbergh, risked their lives and made high drama of the new dimension they were carving in the air. But still, until 1939, flying was a romantic, devil-may-care wonder, confined to a relative handful of hardy individuals. Commercial flight on a large scale was a mere gleam in the eye of men like Howard Hughes.

It took a second major conflict, World War II, from 1939 to 1945, to provoke the imperative that required new concepts from the designers—and created the arena where hundreds of young men and women would learn the expertise demanded by high-speed, high-tech aircraft.

From the start of flight, death has taken its toll. Flying has always been a high-risk adventure. Never, since men first launched themselves into the air, has the new element given up its sacrifice of stolen lives, just as men have never given up the driving urge to go farther, higher, faster. Despite only a fifty-fifty chance of any mission succeeding, *still* the dream draws many more men and women to spaceflight than any program can accommodate. And still, in 1969, when Michael Collins, Buzz Aldrin and Neil Armstrong first took man to the Moon, the skill of piloting, sheer flying ability, was what actually landed the "Eagle" on the Moon's surface. And still, despite technological sophistication undreamed of 30 or 40 years earlier, despite demands on any flyer for levels of performance and competence and the new understanding of computer science not necessary in early aircraft, it is piloting, *human* control of the aircraft—sometimes, indeed, inspired control—that remains the major factor in getting there and back safely. From this rugged breed of individualists came the bush pilots and the astronauts of today.

After America first landed men on the Moon, the Russian space program pushed ahead with plans for eventually creating a permanent space station where men could live. And in 1982 they sent up two men—Valentin Lebedev and Anatoly Berezovoy—to live on Solyut–7 for seven months. This extraordinary feat has been recorded in the diaries of pilot Lebedev, DIARY OF A COSMONAUT: 211 DAYS IN SPACE.

The Bantam AIR & SPACE series will include several titles by or about flyers from all over the world—and about the planes they flew, including World War II, the postwar era of barnstorming and into the jet age, plus the personal histories of many of the world's greatest pilots. Man is still the most important element in flying.

A NOTE ABOUT
THE AUTHOR

Though recognized today as one of this country's most respected automotive journalists, Don Vorderman began his career as an aviation writer in the 1960s, being featured in numerous aviation magazines of the time. "There are few things in this world that delight me as much as an old airplane," he says. Mr. Vorderman began putting together notes for THE GREAT AIR RACES in 1962, and spoke with dozens of the now legendary figures featured in this book, both in Europe and the United States, most of whom are no longer living. "Since childhood I've been enthralled by the mixture of technology, drama, national pride and camaraderie that early air racing represented. I feel truly honored that I was able to meet so many of these extraordinary people."

Mr. Vorderman has flown in a wide assortment of planes, from a much-loved Stearman to World War II bombers to the Grumman F-14 Tomcat, but never a racing aircraft. "Roscoe Turner once let me sit in his 'Meteor,' " he says ruefully, "but unfortunately that's as close as I ever got."

Also the author of a number of automotive books, Mr. Vorderman writes from his home in Stamford, Connecticut.

Here is a preview of the next volume in the Air & Space Series

TO FLY AND FIGHT

by Clarence Anderson

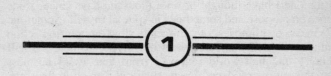

He was someone who was trying to kill me, is all.

THE SKY ABOVE WAS A BRIGHT CRYSTAL blue, and the land below a green-on-green checkerboard divided by a silver-blue ribbon. Below was occupied France, beyond the river lay Germany, and it all looked the same, rolling and peaceful and bursting with spring.

But this was an overpoweringly sinister place. From our perch six miles up, we couldn't see the enemy, some huddling over their guns taking aim, some climbing into their airplanes to fly up and get us, and some, on the far side of the river, waiting with pitchforks and hoping we'd fall somewhere close. All we could see was the green of their fields and forests. But we knew they were there, looking up, watching us come, and thinking how they could kill us.

The day was unusually, incredibly clear. In better times, it would have been a day for splashing through trout streams with fly rods, or driving so fast that some giggling girl would beg you to slow. But these weren't those kinds of times. These were the worst times God ever let happen. And so the trout streams were left to the fish, gasoline was a thing you used sparingly, and it was just one more day for flying and fighting and staying alive, if you could, six miles high over Germany.

Staying alive was no simple thing in the skies over Europe in the spring of 1944. A lot of men couldn't. It was a bad thing to dwell on if you were a fighter pilot, and so we told ourselves we were dead men and lived for the moment with no thought of the future at all. It wasn't too difficult. Lots of us *had* no future and everyone knew it.

This particular day, out of the year I flew combat in Europe, is the one I have thought of on a thousand days since, sometimes on purpose and sometimes in spite of myself. Sometimes it's in cameo glimpses, other times in slow motion stop action, but always in Technicolor. I sit on my porch, nearly a half-century and half-world removed from that awful business, looking out over a deep, green, river-cut canyon to the snow-capped Sierra, thinking about getting tires for the Blazer or mowing the lawn or, more likely, the next backpacking trip . . . and suddenly May 27, 1944, elbows its way to the front of my thoughts like a drunk to a bar. The projectionist inside my head who chooses the films seems to love this one rerun.

We were high over a bomber stream in our P–51B Mustangs, escorting the heavies to the Ludwigshafen-Mannheim area. For the past several weeks the Eighth Air Force had been targeting oil, and Ludwigshafen was a center for synthetic fuels. Oil was everything, the lifeblood of war. Nations can't fight without oil. All through my training, and all through the war, I can't remember ever being limited on how much I could fly. There always was fuel enough. But by 1944, the Germans weren't so fortunate. They were feeling the pinch from the daily bombardments. Without fuel and lubricant, their war machine eventually would grind to a stop. Now that the Mustang fighters were arriving in numbers, capable of escorting the bombers all the way to their targets and back, Germany's oil industry was there for the pounding.

The day would come, and it would be soon, when the German Air Force, the Luftwaffe, would begin picking its spots, contesting some missions and not others; or concentrating on isolated bomber formations, to the exclusion of all the rest, largely at random from what we could tell. The Luftwaffe's idea was to conserve fuel and pilots. But for the moment, at least, there seemed no great shortage of fighter planes between us and the target.

We'd picked up the bombers at 27,000 feet, assumed the right flank, and almost immediately all hell began breaking loose up ahead of us. This was early, still over France, long before we'd expected the German fighters to come up in force. You maintained radio silence until you engaged the enemy, and after that it didn't much matter since they knew you were there, and so people would chatter. They were chattering now, up ahead, and my earphones were crackling with loud, frantic calls: "Bandits, 11 o'clock low! . . . Two o'clock high, pick him up! . . . Blue leader break left!" It sounded as though the Messerschmitts and Focke-Wulfs were everywhere.

You knew how it was up ahead, and you knew it would be like that for you any minute now, the German single-seat Fw 190's and Me 109's coming straight through the bombers, mixing it up with the Mustangs, the hundreds of four-engined heavies and the hundreds of fighters scoring the crystal blue sky with their persistent white contrails.

The Germans liked to roar through the bombers head on, firing long bursts, and then roll and go down. They would circle around to get ahead of the bomber stream, groping for altitude, avoiding the escorts if possible, then reassemble and come through head on again. When their fuel or ammunition was exhausted, they would land and refuel and take off again, flying mission after mission, for as long as there were bombers to shoot at. They seldom came after us. Normally, they would skirmish the escorts only out of necessity. We were an inconvenience, best avoided. It was the bombers they wanted, and the German pilots threw themselves at them smartly and bravely. It was our job to stop them.

It seemed we were always outnumbered. We had more fighters than they did, but what mattered was how many they could put up in one area. They would concentrate in huge numbers, by the hundreds at times. They would assemble way up ahead, pick a section of the bomber formation, and then come in head on, their guns blazing, sometimes hitting the bombers below us before we knew what was happening.

In the distance, a red and black smear marked the spot where a B–17 and its 10 men had been. Planes still bearing their bomb loads erupted and fell, trailing flame, streaking the sky, leaving gaps in the bomber formation that were quickly closed up. Through our headsets we could hear the war, working its way back toward us, coming straight at us at hundreds of miles per hour. The adrenaline began gushing, and I scanned the sky frantically, trying to pick out the fly-speck against the horizon that might have been somebody coming to kill us, trying to see him before he saw me, looking, squinting, breathless . . .

Over the radio: "Here they come!"

They'd worked over the bombers up ahead and now it was our turn.

Things happen quickly. We get rid of our drop tanks, slam the power up, and make a sweeping left turn to engage. My flight of four Mustangs is on the outside of the turn, a wingman close behind to my left, my element leader and his wingman behind to my right, all in finger formation. Open your right hand, tuck the thumb under, put the fingers together, and check the fingernails. That's how we flew, and fought. Two shooters, and two men to cover their tails. The Luftwaffe flew that way, too. German ace Werner Mölders is generally credited with inventing the tactic during the Spanish Civil War.

Being on the outside of the turn, we are vulnerable to attack from the rear. I look over my right shoulder and, sure enough, I see four dots above us, way back, no threat at the moment, but coming hard down the chute. I start to call out, but . . .

"Four bogeys, five o'clock high!" My element leader, Eddie Simpson, has already seen them. *Bogeys* are unknowns and *bandits* are hostile. Quickly, the dots close and take shape. They're hostile, all right. They're Messerschmitts.

We turn hard to the right, pulling up into a tight string formation, spoiling their angle, and we try to come around and go at them head on. The Me 109's change course, charge past, and continue on down, and we wheel and give chase. There are four of them, single-seat fighters, and they pull up, turn hard, and we begin turning with them. We are circling now, tighter and tighter, chasing each other's tails, and I'm sitting there wondering what the hell's happening. These guys want to hang around. Curious. I'm wondering why they aren't after the bombers, why they're messing with us, whether they're simply creating some kind of a diversion or what. I would fly 116 combat missions, engage the enemy perhaps 40 times, shoot down 16 fighters, share in the destruction of a bomber, destroy another fighter on the ground, have a couple of aerial probables, and over that span it would be us bouncing them far more often than not. This was a switch.

We're flying tighter circles, gaining a little each turn, our throttles wide open, 30,000 feet up. The Mustang is a wonderful airplane, 37 feet wingtip to wingtip, just a little faster than the smaller German fighters, and also just a little more nimble. Suddenly the 109's, sensing things are not going well, roll out and run, turning east, flying level. Then one lifts up his nose and climbs away from the rest.

We roll out and go after them. They're flying full power, the black smoke pouring out their exhaust stacks. I'm looking at the one who is climbing, wondering what he is up to, and I'm thinking that if we stay with the other three, this guy will wind up above us. I send Simpson up after him. He and his wingman break off. My wingman, John Skara, and I chase the other three fighters, throttles all the way forward, and I can see that we're gaining.

I close to within 250 yards of the nearest Messerschmitt—dead astern, 6 o'clock, no maneuvering, no nothing—and squeeze the trigger on the control stick between my knees gently. *Bambambambambam!* The sound is loud in the cockpit in spite of the wind shriek and engine roar. And the vibration of the Mustang's four .50-caliber machine guns, two in each wing, weighing 60-odd pounds apiece, is pronounced. In fact, you had to be careful in dogfights when you were turning hard, flying on the brink of a stall, because the buck of the guns was enough to peel off a few critical miles per hour and make the Mustang simply stop flying. That could prove downright embarrassing.

But I'm going like hell now, and I can see the bullets tearing at the Messerschmitt's wing root and fuselage. The armor-piercing ammunition we used was also incendiary, and hits were easily visible, making a bright flash and puff. Now the 109's trailing smoke thickens, and it's something more than exhaust smoke. He slows, and then suddenly rolls over. But the plane doesn't fall. It continues on, upside down, straight and level! What the hell . . . ?

The pilot can't be dead. It takes considerable effort to fly one of these fighter planes upside down. You have to push hard on the controls. Flying upside down isn't easy. It isn't something that happens all by itself, or that you do accidentally. So what in the world is he doing?

Well. It's an academic question, because I haven't the time to wait and and find out. I pour another burst into him, pieces start flying off, I see flame, and the 109 plummets and falls into a spin, belching smoke. My sixth kill.

The other two Messerschmitt pilots have pulled away now, and they're nervous. Their airplanes are twitching, the fliers obviously straining to look over their shoulders and see what is happening. As we take up the chase again, two against two now, the trailing 109 peels away and dives for home, and the leader pulls up into a sharp climbing turn to the left. This one can fly, and he obviously has no thought of running. I'm thinking this one could be trouble.

We turn inside him, my wingman and I, still at long range, and he pulls around harder, passing in front of us right-to-left at an impossible angle. I want to swing in behind him, but I'm going too fast, and figure I would only go skidding on past. A Mustang at speed simply can't make a square corner. And in a dogfight you don't want to surrender your airspeed. I decide to overshoot him and climb.

He reverses his turn, trying to fall in behind us. My wingman is vulnerable now. I tell Skara, "Break off!" and he peels away. The German goes after him, and I go after the German, closing on his tail before he can close on my wingman. He sees me coming and dives away with me after him, then makes a climbing left turn. I go screaming by, pull up, and he's reversing his turn—man, he can fly!—and he comes crawling right up behind me, close enough that I can see him distinctly. He's bringing his nose up for a shot, and I haul back on the stick and climb even harder. I keep going up, because I'm out of alternatives.

This is what I see all these years later. If I were the sort to be troubled with nightmares, this is what would shock me awake. I am in this steep climb, pulling the stick into my navel, making it steeper, steeper . . . and I am looking back down, over my shoulder, at this classic gray Me 109 with black crosses that is pulling up too, steeper, steeper, the pilot trying to get his nose up just a little bit more and bring me into his sights.

There is nothing distinctive about the aircraft, no fancy markings, nothing to identify it as the plane of an ace, as one of the "dreaded yellow-noses" like you see in the movies. Some of them did that, I know, but I never saw one. And in any event, all of their aces weren't flamboyant types who splashed paint on their airplanes to show who they were. I suppose I could go look it up in the archives. There's the chance I could find him in some *gruppe*'s log book, having flown on this particular day, in this particular place, a few miles northwest of the French town of Strasbourg that sits on the Rhine. There are fellows who've done that, gone back and looked up their opponents. I never have. I never saw any point.

He was someone who was trying to kill me, is all.

So I'm looking back, almost straight down now, and I can see this 20-millimeter cannon sticking through the middle of the fighter's propeller hub. In the theater of my memory, it is enormous. An elephant gun. And that isn't far wrong. It is a gun designed to bring down a bomber, one that fires shells as long as your hand, shells that explode and tear big holes in metal. It is the single most frightening thing I have seen in my life, then and now.

But I'm too busy to be frightened. Later on, you might sit back and perspire about it, maybe 40–50 years later, say, sitting on your porch 7,000 miles away, but while it is happening you are just too damn busy. And I am extremely busy up here, hanging by my propeller, going almost straight up, full emergency power, which a Mustang could do for only so long before losing speed, shuddering, stalling, and falling back down; and I am thinking that if the Mustang stalls before the Messerschmitt stalls, I have had it.

I look back, and I can see that he's shuddering, on the verge of a stall. He hasn't been able to get his nose up enough, hasn't been able to bring that big gun to bear. Almost, but not quite. I'm a fallen-down-dead man almost, but not quite. His nose begins dropping just as my airplane, too, begins shuddering. He stalls a second or two before I stall, drops away before I do.

Good old Mustang.

He is falling away now, and I flop the nose over and go after him hard. We are very high by this time, six miles and then some, and falling very, very fast. The Messerschmitt had a head start, plummeting out of my range, but I'm closing up quickly. Then he flattens out and comes around hard to the left and starts climbing again, as if he wants to come at me head on. Suddenly we're right back where we started.

A lot of this is just instinct now. Things are happening too fast to think everything out. You steer with your right hand and feet. The right hand also triggers the guns. With your left, you work the throttle, and keep the airplane in trim, which is easier to do than describe.

Any airplane with a single propeller produces torque. The more horsepower you have, the more the prop will pull you off to one side. The Mustangs I flew used a 12-cylinder Packard

Merlin engine that displaced 1,649 cubic inches. That is 10 times the size of the engine that powers an Indy car. It developed power enough that you never applied full power sitting still on the ground because it would pull the plane's tail up off the runway and the propeller would chew up the concrete. With so much power, you were continually making minor adjustments on the controls to keep the Mustang and its wing-mounted guns pointed straight.

There were three little palm-sized wheels you had to keep fiddling with. They trimmed you up for hands-off level flight. One was for the little trim tab on the tail's rudder, the vertical slab which moves the plane left or right. Another adjusted the tab on the tail's horizontal elevators that raise or lower the nose and help reduce the force you had to apply for hard turning. The third was for aileron trim, to keep your wings level, although you didn't have to fuss much with that one. Your left hand was down there a lot if you were changing speeds, as in combat . . . while at the same time you were making minor adjustments with your feet on the rudder pedals and your hand on the stick. At first it was awkward. But, with experience, it was something you did without thinking, like driving a car and twirling the radio dial.

It's a little unnerving to think about how many things you have to deal with all at once to fly combat.

So the Messerschmitt is coming around again, climbing hard to his left, and I've had about enough of this. My angle is a little bit better this time. So I roll the dice. Instead of cobbing it like before and sailing on by him, I decide to turn hard left inside him, knowing that if I lose speed and don't make it I probably won't get home. I pull back on the throttle slightly, put down 10 degrees of flaps, and haul back on the stick just as hard as I can. And the nose begins coming up and around, slowly, slowly. . . .

Hot damn! I'm going to make it! I'm inside him, pulling my sights up to him. And the German pilot can see this. This time, it's the Messerschmitt that breaks away and goes zooming straight up, engine at maximum power, without much alternative. I come in with full power and follow him up, and the gap narrows swiftly. He is hanging by his prop, not quite vertically, and I am right there behind him, and it is terribly clear, having tested the theory less than a minute ago, that he is going to stall and fall away before I do.

I have him. He must know that I have him.

I bring my nose up, he comes into my sights, and from less than 300 yards I trigger a long, merciless burst with my Brownings. Every fifth bullet or so is a tracer, leaving a thin trail of smoke, marking the path of the bullet stream. The tracers race upward and find him. The bullets chew at the wing root, the cockpit, the engine, making bright little flashes. I hose the Messerschmitt down the way you'd hose down a campfire, methodically, from one end to the other, not wanting to make a mistake here. The 109 shakes like a retriever coming out of the water, throwing off pieces. He slows, almost stops, as if parked in the sky, his propeller just windmilling, and he begins smoking heavily.

My momentum carries me to him. I throttle back to ease my plane alongside, just off his right wing. Have I killed him? I do not particularly want to fight this man again. I am coming up even with the cockpit, and although I figure the less I know about him the better, I find myself looking in spite of myself. There is smoke in the cockpit. I can see that, nothing more. Another few feet. . . .

And then he falls away suddenly, left wing down, right wing rising up, obscuring my view. I am looking at the 109's sky blue belly, the wheel wells, twin radiators, grease marks, streaks from the guns, the black crosses. I am close enough to make out the rivets. The Messerschmitt is right there and then it is gone, just like that, rolling away and dropping its nose and falling (flying?) almost straight down, leaking coolant and trailing flame and smoke so black and thick that it has to be oil smoke. It simply plunges, heading straight for the deck. No spin, not even a wobble, no parachute, and now I am wondering. His ship seems a death ship—but is it?

Undecided, I peel off and begin chasing him down. Did I squander a chance here? Have I let him escape? He is diving hard enough to be shedding his wings, harder than anyone designed those airplane to dive, 500 miles an hour and more, and if 109's will stall sooner than Mustangs going straight up, now I am worrying that maybe their wings stay on longer. At 25,000 feet I begin to grow nervous. I pull back on the throttle, ease out of the dive, and watch him go down. I have no more stomach for this kind of thing, not right now, not with this guy. Enough. Let him go and to hell with him.

Straight down he plunges, from as high as 35,000 feet, through this beautiful, crystal clear May morning toward the green-on-green checkerboard fields, leaving a wake of black smoke. From four miles straight up I watch as the Messerschmitt and the shadow it makes on the ground rush toward one another . . .

. . . and then, finally, silently, merge.

Eddie Simpson joins up with me. Both wingmen, too. Simpson, my old wingman and friend, had gotten the one who'd climbed out. We'd bagged three of the four. We were very excited. It had been a good day.

I had lived and my opponent had died. But it was a near thing. It could have been the other way around just as easily, and what probably made the difference was the airplane I flew. Made in America. I would live to see the day when people would try to tell me the United States can't make cars like some other folks do. What a laugh.

I didn't wonder if I'd just made a new bride a widow, or if he might have had kids, any more than I would have wondered about a snake's mate and offspring. I may have given some thought to how many of my friends he had killed, or might have killed in the future, or how many bombers he might have shot down had he lived. But that's as far as it went. From what I could tell, he hadn't been overly concerned about me.

People ask about that all the time. People usually ask it hesitantly, as tactfully as they can, but they ask it. Did I wonder and worry about the mothers and children and wives of the men I shot down? Did I carry any guilt or regret?

No.

Not then, and not now.

World War Two was a total thing, *us against them*, when being against *them* was unquestionably the right thing to be. I flew for my country, and was proud I could help in any way that I could.

Besides, all of my opponents were trying to kill me. And frankly, I always was elated they hadn't.

This one had almost gotten a bead on me. He'd come as close as anyone would. When it was done, the 480 hours of combat flying in P–51s, and another 25 or so missions in Vietnam, almost all of those in F–105s, I never once suffered a hit in air-to-air combat. The sum total of the damage all my aircraft absorbed amounted to one small-arms round that found one of my wings during a strafing run after D-Day. It bored a hole the size of my little finger. It didn't even go all the way through, just punctured the underside's skin. Nobody noticed it until the next day. Needing a patch the size of a coin, that's exactly what my crew used—a British shilling.

People on the ground often shot at me. Flak batteries. Machine gunners. Foot soldiers with rifles and pistols. There may have been some who threw rocks, who can say? But this man, on that day, was the only opponent who was ever behind me, and he couldn't quite bring me into his sights, and never did fire.

To my knowledge, I never was fired upon by an airplane in combat.

Skill had something to do with that, I suppose. But there was certainly something more to it than skill. Lots of hot pilots never came home. I guess I was lucky. Or blessed.

That night, back at our Leiston base, in the "half-pipe" Nissen hut where the flight leaders bunked, we stoked our little stove with coke and made toasted cheese sandwiches. And afterward, after twirling the poker through the coals until it glowed, we ceremonially burned two more little swastikas beneath my name on the hut's wooden door.

O'Bee O'Brien's name was up there, Ed Hiro's, Jim Browning's, Don Bochkay's, Daddy Rabbit Peters'. Chuck Yeager, who three years later would become the first man to fly through the sound barrier, would have his name up there too, along with some others. Already, there were a lot of little swastikas burned into that door. Fortunately, there was still lots of room. It would be a long war.

There would be a lot more.

Letter from the late Don Bochkay, former commander, 363rd Fighter Squadron, of the 357th Fighter Group, Eighth Air Force, to Lloyd Zacharie, another veteran of the 357th, who was thinking of visiting his old fighter base . . .

☆

Jan. 8, 1980

Dear Zack,

If you go to England and on to Leiston, don't be too disappointed in what you don't see.

I was there on our base in 1970. I was looking for a door off our hut that had a record of kills for Yeager, Browning, Anderson, Peters and myself. Burned in with a hot poker.

I would have given $500 for that door. I didn't find it. I still have a hunch it exists.

Our base at Leiston was being chewed up by a concrete eater when I drove up on one of the runways. No one but us knows the feeling that went through me when I drove up on the active runway to see the big monsters destroying our base.

I relived a thousand days as I looked down that main runway, (thought) of boys who became men and did what they had to do, men who backed them to the hilt with their skills to make it possible.

I shed my tears at Leiston when I was there in '70, and I will remember it forever.

Have a good trip if you go to Leiston, and don't be ashamed to cry.

Yours,
Don

*I remember the incredible, intoxicating
smell of the gasoline, oil and airplane
dope, like a new car smell . . .*

THE PLANE HAD GONE DOWN ON THE Martin Ranch, less than
three miles away, and we were quick getting to it. The foothills
west of the High Sierra are full of abrupt little rises, and on a
dark, misting December evening the big Boeing biplane had
found one, abruptly.

It was a new Model 80 tri-motor, capable of carrying 12
passengers and a thousand pounds of mail. A year later, another
Model 80 would become the first aircraft to carry a stewardess.
There had been only four aboard this one on the night of
December 18, 1929, flying the Reno-to-Oakland mail run: the
pilot, co-pilot, and two passengers. The pilot, who said he'd
flown fighters in World War I (an ace, the papers reported),
had set it down nicely, or luckily, and all had survived.

Flying from here to there in an airliner was still an adventure
in 1929. Planes had a tendency to fly into things, and when
they did they tended to fold up like papier-mache and often
caught fire. Crashes generally weren't something you walked
away from whistling. And then, as now, plunging into orchard
country in fog was risky business. The *Sacramento Bee* thought
this significant: "Mrs. Sullivan . . . has traveled much by airplane . . . It is reported last night's crash was her first air mishap."

We bounded out of my parents' car almost before it had
stopped the next morning, eager to sift through the wreckage.
The papers were full of the "giant" airliner's crash, and the
whole town turned out. The local high school even sent a
busload of kids from the auto mechanics class. Jack Stacker

and I entered the plane, examining the cabin and twisted cockpit methodically. We selected some pieces we found on the ground and carried them off. I kept mine for years, as if they were treasure.

I was just shy of eight, Jack barely seven.

And after that, all we talked and dreamed of were airplanes and airplanes and airplanes.

I don't remember ever *not* knowing Jack, a tall, thin, big-eyed youngster with the ever-ready grin and charisma of a good used car salesman. Our parents were friends from before we were born. We played together, were Boy Scouts together, fished and shot and hunted together, competed in sports together, negotiated steep serpentine roads on a motorcycle together, drank and smoked and girlwatched together when the time came for that, and dreamed and talked bravely of flying together.

When I finally did get my pilot's license, I gave Jack his very first ride, in a two-place J–3 Cub. He threw up.

We grew up a few miles apart, a half-hour's drive out of Sacramento, California, northeast into the foothills. I lived near a place called Newcastle, a town of 1,000 just up the hill from where Jack lived in Loomis. With the freeways they have now, it is another five minutes to Auburn, and an hour to the pass through the mountains, 7,200 feet up. There, in 1846, the Donner wagon train bogged down in a fearful blizzard, with half the party either freezing or starving and the rest turning cannibal. Just beyond, the road to the east plunges and forks to Lake Tahoe or Reno.

It is some of the loveliest country on the face of the planet, pine-forested over and laced with Indian trails. Along one, from Squaw Valley down to Auburn, two world-renowned 100-mile races are contested each year. One is on horseback, the other on foot. You can run the 100 miles in less than 18 hours if you're trained and determined enough. You can do almost anything if you're trained and determined.

Foothill summers are dry, hot and brown, the winters wet, chilly and green, with most free of snow. It was gold-rush country midway through the last century—hard, cruel country with quick, angry justice, a place where some dreams came true and more didn't; where stagecoaches hauled the gold and people named Rattlesnake Dick and Black Bart made a good living robbing them; where men were men and women were something you ordered by mail.

There are still mines all over, most abandoned, some not. The price of the metal goes up, and here and there mines reopen. People still pan for pin-money gold in the rivers and streams. But when we were growing up, what more people mined were the fruit trees that thrived there—apple, cherry, nectarine, peach, plum, pomegranate and pear.

My father, Clarence Emil Anderson, Sr., a hardy and determined old Swede, had a few hundred acres given over to orchard. He had cleared and planted the land, and did nicely until the Depression, when the bigger farms in the valley drove him to bankruptcy and he lost almost everything. He saved the homestead with government loans and by selling off pieces of land, just like the neighbors did.

I was into my teens while all that was happening, but was never really aware. There was always food enough, and if noodles and tiny meatballs in water came advertised as soup a couple of nights in a row, it wasn't a thing to complain about. There was always fresh clothing for school. For awhile there were always new cars, and then there weren't, but I never knew why. My parents never burdened me with their problems. I only found out years later.

My kid brother David, a librarian at the University of California at Davis, still lives in our parents' large, two-story white house. He raised a family there. But the orchards, ours and the others, are almost all gone now. The countryside around Newcastle is a bedroom community for burgeoning Sacramento, thick with large, trendy houses. Newcastle itself, where the fruit was hauled to be packed and shipped east, was a busy little rail center in those days, living off the area's farms. Now, the downtown area is the next thing to a ghost town, with the packing sheds converted into gift and antique shops and restaurants. Still, it presses on stubbornly.

Dreams have always died hard there.

I was the third of my father's four children, born January 13, 1922, in Oakland, where my Mom's parents lived. Friday the 13th, it was. If it's an unlucky day, you couldn't prove it by me. I've been pretty lucky. I never was superstitious.

It says Clarence Emil Anderson, Jr., on my birth certificate, but few call me Clarence or Junior and none call me Emil. When I was young, my family nicknamed me Buddy, which in time became Bud. The men I flew with used Andy, because all Andersons are automatically Andy. In the service, of course, you're often called by your rank, Lieutenant, Captain, Major, or Colonel. By now, I answer to just about anything. I live in Auburn now, in a house with someone else's name on the mailbox (my father-in-law's). For years, there was still another name over the doorbell (my wife's grandmother's). The house itself, built in 1888 by a Civil War officer, is written up in a book about the city's old houses with no mention at all of the people who live there today. If I had an identity crisis, you could understand why.

The very first thing I remember is Lindbergh making it across the Atlantic when I was just five. I have no idea why somebody flying from one place to another should have made such a lasting impression, but it kindled an interest in airplanes that would last for a lifetime. When I was seven, my father took me to Sacramento, to a little dirt airfield with one little hangar where a fellow named Ingvald Fagerskog made or supplemented his living by taking people up for rides in a Stearman biplane. The airfield was on Auburn Boulevard, near Watt Avenue. I can remember being excited and a little bit frightened, the incredible, intoxicating smells of the gasoline, oil, and airplane dope, like a new car smell; and the throaty sound of the engine. Most of all I remember flying over our house and circling tightly, the pilot standing the plane on its side.

There were two open cockpits, with goggled Ingvald in back and Dad and I in the front, and wires running all over the place, strut-to-strut, bracing the wings. My father pointed straight down at the farm, hollering over the little Wright Whirlwind radial's roar and the shriek of wind in the wires, and I sat staring down at my shoes, trying to work up the courage to turn and look out.

I know it was May 11, 1929, and I know Ingvald Fagerskog's unlikely name, because while rummaging through my late mother's trunk in researching this book I came across a yellowed certificate bearing these details. Why she preserved it for half a century, I really can't say. As far as I know, it was my father's first ride as well, one of the few flights he ever took in the 80-odd years that he lived, and what made him drive 60 miles round-trip to do it with his young son in tow is anyone's guess. I suppose that my interest in airplanes was reason enough.

The history of man in flight....

THE BANTAM AIR AND SPACE SERIES

The Bantam Air and Space Series is dedicated to the men and women who brought about this, the era of flight -- the century in which mankind not only learned to soar the skies, but has journeyed out into the blank void of space.

☐ 1: THE LAST OF THE BUSH PILOTS
     by Harmon Helmericks   28556-4 $4.95

☐ 2: FORK TAILED DEVIL: THE P-38
     by Martin Caidin   28557-2 $4.95

☐ 3: THE FASTEST MAN ALIVE
     by Frank Everest and John Guenther 28771-0 $4.95

☐ 4: DIARY OF A COSMONAUT: 211 DAYS IN
     SPACE by Valentin Lebedev   28778-8 $4.95

☐ 5: FLYING FORTS by Martin Caidin 28780-X $4.95

☐ 6: ISLAND IN THE SKY
     by Ernest K. Gann   28857-1 $4.95

☐ 7: PILOT
     by Tony Le Vier with John Guenther   28785-0 $4.95

☐ 8: BARNSTORMING
     by Martin Caidin   28818-0 $4.95

☐ 9: THE ELECTRA STORY: AVIATION'S
     GREATEST MYSTERY by Robert J. Serling
                        28845-8 $4.95

Available now wherever Bantam Falcon Books are sold, or use this page for ordering: